NO MATTER WHAT
YOU CAN DO IT

Success is Not Difficult,
But Requires Relentless Pursuit

Red O'Laughlin

D1569723

NO MATTER WHAT YOU CAN DO IT

Copyright © 2017 by MRO GLOBAL, LLC

ISBN 9781520782058

Dedication

NO MATTER WHAT YOU CAN DO IT is dedicated to my wife, Marilyn O'Laughlin, for her support throughout this entire process. She has spent countless hours supporting, cajoling, reading, editing and keeping me focused.

I also recognize my mentor, Myron Golden, for his advice and encouragement.

Table of Contents

Preface

This book provides information that can be used immediately. The user will find that he or she can change significantly within 21 days if the right steps are taken. Many texts, CDs and self-improvement programs tell us 'what' to do or 'how' to do it, but usually not the 'why.' I believe if you know 'why' something works or doesn't work, then you have a higher probability of success. This book includes the 'why.'

I developed the idea of **'NO MATTER WHAT'** from the book *Psycho-Cybernetics* by Maxwell Maltz. Your subconscious mind has a tremendous effect on you, and you can control it to make you better. You must make that decision – to remain as you are - or - to live the life of your dreams.

Hence, once you decide to do something – *NO MATTER WHAT!* - you can achieve most anything you want. However, just saying it once doesn't make it happen. You must be relentless in your pursuit. Otherwise, you have reinforced failure into your subconscious mind and it will become easier to fail in the future.

Failure happens in many aspects of our lives – spiritual, financial, health, relationships, etc. We didn't learn what we needed to be successful. Or, we didn't apply what we did learn. Action, consistent action is required for success.

You have a **95% probability of financial failure** – YES – FAILURE - in achieving financial stability for your retirement years. A very dismal statistic, but true! Many of you can, but do not take the necessary actions to achieve a healthy and wealthy lifestyle that you truly need to be happy in your later years.

Introduction

Red O'Laughlin became a real student of motivation and self-improvement because of attending a training session hosted by Jeffrey Combs and Myron Golden in Houston, Texas in November 2006. Although I had been well educated (five college degrees and six professional certifications), I was never fully exposed to the field of personal development and self-improvement.

In January 2007, I started reading personal development and self-improvement books, magazines and articles. I set my initial goal of reading one book a week on personal growth and self-improvement and maintained that rate for over three and a half years. Additionally, I have listened to over hundreds of CDs and watched dozens of DVDs; and, attended many seminars to improve my knowledge in personal growth, self-development and motivation. I have studied and analyzed the works of the masters, the current gurus and have interviewed many of today's entrepreneurial leaders for additional insight.

Failure comes easy and quitting comes easier if you do not know how your subconscious mind controls you. Some people will swear that diets do not work. The reality is most diets work, people do not. The choices you make today determine your successes tomorrow. Choices have consequences. If you haven't been feeding your brain the nourishment it needs to grow, then now is the time to fertilize and plants those seeds for your success. This book will discuss, in detail, how you can wrestle control away from your subconscious mind and train it to work for you to achieve the goals in your life.

Over the course of my study on personal growth and motivation, I heard a story that has stayed with me. A young student sought fame, glory and success in his life. He traveled the country looking for wisdom. One day he approached an old master and asked him if he could show him the secret to success. The old master looked at the young man and studied him for a minute, then said, *"Yes, I can. Follow me."* He led the young man to the back of his garden and got down on one knee and pointed into the pond and said, *"The secret to success is right there."*

The young student got down on his knee and studied the water. He could not see anything unusual. He said, *"Master, I see nothing but water and pebbles."* The master said, *"You must look closer!"* The young student now got down on both his knees and really concentrated on what might be just below the surface of the pond. The young student again told the master, *"Master, I cannot see the secret of success in life."*

The old master took his finger and gently pushed it into the water a little way and told the young student, *"It is right here. Certainly, you must see it!"* The young student bent a little closer to the water and suddenly, the old master grabbed the back of his neck and pushed his head under water. He held the young student's head in the water while the young man thrashed about and tried to get his head out of the water.

After several seconds of holding the young man's head under the water, the old master released his grip and allowed the young man to regain his senses. The old master told the young man, *"If you put the same effort into anything you do, as you just did to get your head out of the water, you will become a success in anything you do."*

Success comes from a lot of hard work and effort. However, there are smarter ways of achieving success. You will learn those smart ways of achieving success from this book. You can start, here and now, with your first **NO MATTER WHAT** decision – to capture your thoughts as they apply to what you want to achieve in your life; and, more importantly, <u>how you are going to achieve</u>

them. The lessons you will learn and the skills you will develop from this book will provide you with the tools you need to overcome any obstacle in your path to living the life of your dreams.

Throughout this book, I have provided examples of **NO MATTER WHAT** decisions that have been made which I consider being 'above and beyond' the typical **NO MATTER WHAT** decision one might make to go to college, excel in sports, attain a promotion, buy a new home, etc. Every one of these **NO MATTER WHAT** decisions was extremely important to the individual, team, organization or nation at the time. All of them are inspiring and truly noteworthy. Please enjoy the ones I have selected.

"Experience is a hard teacher. She gives the test first and the lesson afterward." Dick Enberg

"I am a great believer in luck, and I find the harder I work, the more I have of it." Thomas Jefferson

"Always do your best. What you plant now, you will harvest later." Og Mandino

"If you want something you've never had, you have to do something you've never done." Mike Murdock

"It's been my observation that most people get ahead during the time other people waste." Henry Ford

No Matter What You Can Do It

"What your mind can conceive and believe you can achieve." W. Clement Stone

"Our self-image, strongly held, essentially determines what we become." Maxwell Maltz

"For as he thinketh in his heart, so is he." Proverbs 23:7

"The price of success is much lower than the price of failure." Thomas Watson

"What you believe about you, impacts you more than what others believe about you." Bill Bartmann

No Matter What You Can Do It

Preamble

There are many ways to make positive and permanent changes in your life. I will highlight a few of those processes that I have found to be beneficial and relatively easy to master. Towards the end of this book, I will identify some suggestions for additional sources of income to help you on your quest for financial freedom. In the end, it is about controlling what 'you have' and what 'you can do' to attain your dreams. The final choice is always yours.

"You can't think and act like a victim and expect victory."
Bill Bartmann

"Action creates motivation." Zig Ziglar

"Men willingly believe what they wish." Julius Caesar

"Luck is what happens when preparation meets opportunity."
Seneca

"I never worry about action, but only about inaction."
Winston Churchill

No Matter What You Can Do It

Mindset

Every day we see books and magazine articles on how to prepare for our retirement - *"Invest in these Top 20 stocks"*, *"Double your portfolio value by using these insider-trading secrets"*, *"Live in luxury with our simple six-step system"*, etc. We are constantly bombarded with methods and systems for creating, or accumulating, more wealth in our lives – particularly aimed at our retirement years. However, the secret they don't tell you is that to truly <u>attain and keep</u> – the operative word here is 'keep', you <u>must change</u> yourself – your mindset.

Why do so many lottery winners, sports professionals and many celebrities end their lives without the benefits of the wealth they acquired during their lives? They <u>never became</u> the person they should have become to handle their newly acquired wealth. I am talking about the <u>mindset</u> you <u>must acquire</u> to keep the wealth and financial freedom you desire.

No Matter What You Can Do It

This book will give you the basics to take that 'first step' in changing your mindset so that you can keep what you have; and, attain that little bit extra that will make a major difference in your life. Statistical analyses show us that an extra $200 to $400 a month would have prevented 80% of the bankruptcies over the past ten years. That is not a lot of money.

We must change ourselves to become better stewards of our lives. I remember when I was making $300 a month and spending $305 a month. That was before credit cards came into vogue, and it required carefully paying some bills a little later than I should have. As I got older, I found out that I could easily live on $3000 a month by spending $3100 a month. Now, my debt was starting to climb, but if I made monthly payments rather than paying off the whole balance, I was safe – so I thought.

I will take you through a series of options for your consideration to begin your transition into your prosperity mindset – one that will afford you the luxury of living a better lifestyle without having to watch your debt rocket out of sight. You must make up your mind to change yourself to make it happen. This is not impossible, nor difficult, only different. You do not need a college education to make the change – you just need the desire to do it. It is all in your mind already – just wake it up and use it! It is not a quick and easy financial formula. Every one of us can do it, but less than <u>five</u> percent of us invest the time and energy to do it.

Morris Massey is a world-renowned trainer. I have been fortunate to talk with him socially and listen to several of his training sessions. He says that we generally will not change unless there is a Significant Emotional Event in our lives. Sometimes that Significant Emotional Event happens to us – such as a 'near miss' that would have resulted in our death or disability. Other times it happens to a family member or very close friend. We suddenly see what could happen to us if we 'stayed the course' and made no changes in our lives.

After an exposure to a Significant Emotional Event, we can see the <u>need to change</u> and we make that conscious decision to change - we <u>now have the reason</u> and resolve to change. This reason to change has <u>emotion</u> attached to it - which filters through our mind differently and stays with us – almost like a guiding light. Emotion establishes more emphasis on this goal than on previous goals you have made. It becomes your **NO MATTER WHAT** decision.

In his book, *Awaken the Giant Within*, Anthony Robbins tells us that making a '<u>decision</u>' is critical to change. We associate our decisions with <u>pain or pleasure</u>. We either avoid pain or want to gain pleasure. Even though we know what to do, we do not do it – we miss the opportunity because we associate or desire less pain to **not** do it -- than to <u>do it</u>. Lasting change requires <u>long-range focus and commitment</u>. In this book, I will explore and provide guidance to assist you in making those decisions required to make a positive change in your lifestyle.

Do not scratch through your To-Do List, your written milestones and goals; but, instead, write the word, **VICTORY**, next to it to start your success mindset change. You need to recognize that what you have done in the past <u>has not worked</u> and it is insanity to keep doing the same thing and expect change. I think Anthony Robbins has hit it on the head - many of us keep stating **preferences** instead of really **making decisions**. We would <u>like to do this</u>, instead of doing <u>it</u>. So, how do you convert your preferences to become actual changes in your lives? Sometimes this conversion comes through utter frustration and despair and sometimes it comes through education and diligence. You can see the path to change, and you must decide that '**NO MATTER WHAT**, I will do it!'

I saw a term the other day that I liked called the 'Poverty Industrial Complex.' It made me think – if there is a Poverty Industrial Complex then there should be a Prosperity Industrial Complex. I thought about the sheer vastness and complexity of our Military Industrial Complex and saw an analogy to our everyday lives. Most of us live in an <u>environment</u> that keeps us from <u>breaking free of its borders</u>. I view the Poverty Industrial

Complex as living in a small country that provides for all your needs. You go to school there, your family lives there, your friends live nearby, you work there, your church is there, and you take your vacations in the usual places each year. Everything you need is in front of you.

There is no horizon in this country. It is always hazy – no clear distinction between the sky and the land or ocean – just a blurry merger. There might be something just on the other side of the horizon, but you cannot see it. You might know or think it is there, but it seems **unapproachable**.

If you were in a helicopter looking at the Poverty Industrial Complex below, you would see a large herd of people - all following each other - with very few straying away from the herd. The herd is comfortable and moves from one grazing spot to another. For whatever reasons - it is very difficult to break away from the herd. The Poverty Industrial Complex provides safety and security for its residents but does not provide financial freedom and a life of your dreams.

Your comfort zone gives you more pleasure compared to the pain of the unknown – of change. Occasionally you see successful people – or the things they acquired during their lives – their homes, their cars, boats and airplanes. What did they do to get those things? Who did they know? Why can't I have some of their luck?

No Matter What You Can Do It

The difference is that they chose – they 'made a decision' to do something to improve their lives. Moreover, once that decision was made, they had the 'focus' to continue that path until they achieved it. They made their **NO MATTER WHAT** decision.

In 2008, Tiger Woods won the 108th US Open Golf Tournament in Torrey Pines, California. He entered the tournament with some major knee and leg problems – damaged anterior cruciate ligament in his left knee and two stress fractures in his left tibia. His doctor told him that he could not damage his leg any more than it was, but the pain would be tremendous. Tiger told his doctor that he was going to <u>play</u> and <u>win</u> the US Open tournament.

Anyone watching him walk the course could see the pain he suffered from every step. Tiger Woods had a <u>goal</u>; he made his **NO MATTER WHAT** decision and kept his <u>focus</u> to achieve it. His victory is like one nearly 60 years ago when Ben Hogan won the 1950 US Open at Merion – also in an 18-hole playoff. Ben Hogan had nearly been killed 16 months previously when a Greyhound bus hit his car head-on. The doctors doubted he would survive, much less walk. However, Ben Hogan had his <u>goal</u>, he made his **NO MATTER WHAT** decision and he kept his <u>focus</u> to achieve his goal to win the US Open.

You might think that Tiger Woods and others are professionals and they do this for a living – certainly, you <u>could not expect me</u>

to have the same ability as them. Not only are they professional athletes, but they are at the <u>top of their competition</u> – who could expect me to <u>compete at that level</u>? You have the same decision-making processes that Tiger Woods and Ben Hogan used. You have it a little better than Ben Hogan had in his day because today we understand how we work much better than we did back in the late 40's and early 50's. It was not until 1950 that we started to truly understand our subconscious mind and how we can program it to make us better.

Morris Goodman wrote the book, *The Miracle Man*. It is his story of personal achievement and self-motivation – the **NO MATTER WHAT** decisions he made. Morris Goodman is a self-made man, a highly successful man by any measure. One of his dreams was to buy and fly his own airplane. He achieved that dream. One day while flying, something happened that changed his life. He crashed.

Morris broke his neck and many other bones. The doctors doubted he would make it through the night. Certainly, if he did – he would live in a vegetative state for the rest of his life. There were too many physical things wrong with him. However, they underestimated his <u>brain</u> – <u>the power of his subconscious mind</u>. Morris had always been self-motivated, made decisions and focused on those things necessary to accomplish them.

Now he had a new decision to make – to accept the doctors' diagnoses; or, to overcome his paralysis and inability to breathe and speak, and get up and walk out of the hospital under his own power. Morris did not want to live a life of a vegetable - he wanted to regain the <u>full use</u> of his body – that was his **NO MATTER WHAT** decision.

He was unable to speak, eat or move. He could not breathe without the use of a respirator. He concentrated on the muscles needed to inhale. Little by little, he could take one breath – or he thought he had. He kept up his mental focus to make his chest muscles work rather than let the machine do the work for him. Soon he could take two breaths in a row – then three and four, and soon he could breathe on his own.

He had a regimen of daily positive thinking. He developed a plan to eat, to talk, to walk, and to live a life as near to normal as possible. He listened to motivational tapes daily, particularly those from Bob Proctor, Zig Ziglar and Norman Vincent Peale. He told himself, *"If I can take one step, I can take a thousand steps. If I can say one word, I can say all words."* He broke each word, each syllable down into its basic functions and concentrated on accomplishing that goal. As he began to chew and swallow on his own, he gained more strength.

Despite the hospital and medical staffs' negativity constantly bombarding him during his recovery process, he managed to breathe on his own and talk within three months. Within a year, he was walking and living at home. After two years, he could hunt and fish again.

Summary:

Your 1st **NO MATTER WHAT** decision is to capture your thoughts by writing them down.

Your 2nd **NO MATTER WHAT** decision is to invest the time required to improve your life.

Your 3rd **NO MATTER WHAT** decision is to make the decision now to do what you need to do and to keep focused on your goal.

- **Guideline #1**: You must change yourself <u>to attain</u> and <u>to keep</u> the freedom and lifestyle you desire.

- $200-400 a month could have prevented 80% of the bankruptcies in the United States in the past ten years.

- Everyone can change, but less than 5% commit to making a change for the better in their lives.

- A decision to change may happen because of a Significant Emotional Event in your life, or in the life of someone close to you.

- A decision may be made based on the pain or pleasure associated with the change. Most people avoid pain rather than select pleasure to make changes in their lives.

- **Guideline #2**: Attach emotion to your decision to make it easier for you to make that change in your life.

- **Guideline #3**: Write VICTORY next to your accomplishments rather than crossing through them.

- **Guideline #4**: Long-range focus and commitment are required for lasting change.

- The Poverty Industrial Complex keeps you from breaking free from its borders.

- Your comfort zone provides you pleasure.

- Successful people make decisions, focus on them and follow through with <u>whatever it takes</u> to achieve their goals.

- **Guideline #5**: Program your subconscious mind to make you better.

"To hit a target, first, you must see it clearly." Bill Bartmann

"I don't know the secret to success, but the key to failure is to try to please everyone." Bill Cosby

"The indispensable first step to getting the things you want out of life is this: decide what you want." Ben Stein

Prosperity Industrial Complex

I mentioned in the last chapter the terms 'Poverty Industrial Complex' and 'Prosperity Industrial Complex'. We know a lot about our Military Industrial Complex – how it permeates many levels of our government and society. It needs to be complex if you are buying and maintaining fleets of aircraft around the world, replacing aging weapons systems, training new recruits, updating technologies and ensuring integration among our military services and our allies – it must be complex.

Fortunately, the military industrial process has <u>made mistakes</u> and <u>learned from them</u>. They have written procedures for many of the tasks that must be done to ensure standardization. They have trained people to perform these tasks. They know their constraints and they know what they must do at designated times. The complexities are astounding when you stop to think about them. Nevertheless, they happen routinely and in the same manner by experienced personnel, as well as the newly trained recruits, regardless of where they work.

Like the Military Industrial Complex, you live every day of your life in either the Poverty Industrial Complex or the Prosperity Industrial Complex. Both are comprised of your educational systems, your work environment, your peers, your family, your expectations, etc. They influence what you think and what you do. The critical difference between the Poverty Industrial Complex and the Prosperity Industrial Complex is the <u>decisions you make</u> about your lives.

In the Poverty Industrial Complex, you do not know what is constraining you or how to combat these constraints. You readily accept the things that the world gives you. If you knew the rules of conduct, the boundaries and your destination – a destination that would allow you to escape from the Poverty Industrial Complex - then you could find your way out – so to speak. I view both the Poverty Industrial Complex and the Prosperity Industrial Complex as a **mindset** – not a **financial state**.

The Poverty Industrial Complex is a mindset that allows you to be comfortable living at the edge of your financial ability. You stretch your lifestyle with credit card debt and reduced/minimal savings. It is the comfort of <u>staying where you are</u> rather than accepting the <u>pain of change</u>. Many rich people have a poverty mindset. **Money is not the key to escape**. If you can <u>change</u> your **mindset** – you can <u>change</u> your **lifestyle!**

Your mindset has been programmed since you were an infant. You have been programmed by your parents, your teachers, your religious leaders, your friends, your co-workers, the music you listened to, the books you read, the television shows you watched, etc. Your parents probably contributed the most to your current self-image.

Maybe you do not know enough information right now to determine if they do or do not have a poverty mindset. As you go through this book, you will better understand a poverty mindset and how to change it.

In the book, *Alice in Wonderland,* by Lewis Carroll, Alice is walking down the road and suddenly comes to several forks in the road and must decide as to which road to take. She sees a Cheshire Cat sitting in a tree on the side of the road. She asks the Cheshire Cat, *"Which road shall I take?"* The Cheshire Cat asks Alice, *"Where are you going?"* Alice says, *"I don't really know."* Then the Cheshire Cat tells Alice, *"It doesn't matter which road you take because any road will get you there."*

Many of us are like Alice – we really do not know where we are going; nor, do we know which road to take. Why is that? Take a better look at the Poverty Industrial Complex. Imagine yourself back in that helicopter flying over the Poverty Industrial Complex.

No Matter What You Can Do It

You might see many hot air balloons. Many of those hot air balloons would be fully deflated. The people in them are stuck – they cannot move. They may not even recognize that filling their balloon with hot air would get them to another location. It just does not dawn on them that they are stuck.

There are some balloons partially inflated, but their balloons have not moved yet. They are taking some action to move to a better location in life. A few hot air balloons are marginally making headway – just a few inches off the ground. Occasionally, you see a hot air balloon taking off and departing the hodge-podge of balloons destined to remain caught in the quagmire of a poverty mindset.

You have been programmed all your lives to accept certain things. The average 18-year old has been told NO at least **80,000 times** in his or her life in some form or another –

- *"NO!"*
- *"Not Now!"*
- *"Sit Down and Be Quiet!"*
- *"We Can't Afford It!"*
- *"Do You Think Money Grows on Trees?"*

You have all heard these terms before and maybe used them yourselves. They linger on in your lives as slogans –

- *"We Can't Afford It!"*

- *'That's What the Rich Do and We're Not Rich!"*

And on and on and on!

Negativity programs your minds to be <u>minimal</u> rather than reach out and grow larger. If you tell a kid, repeatedly, he can never achieve something - <u>he will **never** disappoint you.</u>

Henry Ford said, *"Whether you believe you can do a thing or not, you are right."*

If your value systems (in your subconscious mind) are programmed to **accept what you are** then you will **never exceed** the goals **others set for you**.

Negativity is so pervasive that it literally eats up most of your lives and you <u>do not even recognize</u> it for what it is. **80%** of what you hear, see and read – particularly on TV, is negative programming. It emphasizes the negative aspects of life. Almost 20% of our daily experiences can be viewed as neutral. So, you end up with over 99% of what you see, hear and read keeping you in a negative or disempowering frame of mind – unable to see a bright and vibrant future.

So, how do you break free from your Poverty Industrial Complex or your poverty mindset? Recognize that the negativity in your life is not benefitting you is a <u>start</u> – the first start in your life to a better life for you and your family. How do you break free from the Poverty Industrial Complex and begin building your

Prosperity Industrial Complex? It is easy to describe, but difficult to accomplish. Not difficult because it is impossible, but difficult since you must leave your comfort zone – the one re-enforced by constant negativity – and enter the world in which you make the decisions and focus on what you want in life.

Here is an easy way to start. **Recognize negativity for what it is. Do not allow negativity to have an emotional effect on you.**

For example, assume for a minute that you become upset when you see a red ball. All day long red balls are rolling by you. Sometimes they smack up against you. Each time you see a red ball, you grow a little uneasy. Black balls, blue balls, green balls also go by, but they do not bother you – only the red balls have an effect – something that triggers an internal reaction. Most of the time, you can handle yourself, but occasionally you must tell someone that the last red ball really upset you. I realize that this sounds peculiar.

However, if we viewed these red balls for what they are – red balls, and say – *'Oh, another red ball – not important, I will just ignore it.'* Then you are recognizing negativity for what it is and not allowing it to enter your emotional life. To program the negativity out of your life, you must recognize it and minimize it, without allowing it to evoke any disempowering emotions. Then begin programming positivity into your daily life.

No Matter What You Can Do It

There is also a subtle re-enforcement of our inner personal negativity that many of us share with others daily. It is the response we give to the greeting, *"How are you?"* It is subtle and it constantly re-enforces our internal core belief about ourselves. When asked, *"How are you doing?"* some of us answer, *"Not bad"*; or, *"It could be better."*

Heard those answers before? All of you probably have used these responses at some time in your lives. But, you did not recognize them for what they were – a negative re-enforcement of our own personal value system in your brains – a restriction on what you can do and what you can become.

It will not be easy to remember to give a positive response when asked, *"How are you?"* You have become programmed to give a response – something that you are unaware of and something that becomes mechanical to you over time. You do not think about it.

Make positive responses **(Great! Couldn't be better! Fantastic!)** for the next 21 days when asked, *"How are you?"* It will feel uncomfortable and strange, but it will take another three weeks before it becomes natural.

When you do not feel good – emotionally or physically – responding positively begins to change something within you. You will feel a shift towards the positive. It makes you aware of your current emotional or physical state and helps you to re-focus on spreading positivity in your world.

Recognize what you are reading, listening to and watching for the negativity it contains. When you recognize something for what it is, you are beginning that process of preventing the negativity from re-enforcing your current mindset.

Keep a positive attitude! How many times have you heard that? Did you ever 'realize' that <u>attitude</u> <u>determines</u> so many things in your life? Without a positive attitude, it is so easy to give up and return to the Poverty Industrial Complex where most of you live in **comfort** and **pseudo-security**. Keeping a positive attitude is very challenging and it requires **continual** re-enforcement and training.

When you have a destination - a goal you want to achieve – **<u>visualize the satisfaction</u>** you will have from attaining it. It will help you generate the will to continue your quest. It will keep you <u>focused</u>. The satisfaction of completing your goal will help you to <u>recognize</u> when you have <u>lost focus.</u> That satisfaction will help you concentrate again on your **goal/dream**. I mentioned the focus that Tiger Woods and Ben Hogan used in achieving their goals. It is the same 'focus' - and you can do it if you want to **<u>NO MATTER WHAT!</u>**

Visualization is a very powerful tool for you to change your life. Setting a goal is a good start. Visualizing accomplishing that goal – how you will feel when it is accomplished – the joy of making it – affects you emotionally and attaches a greater need to achieve it – a **NO MATTER WHAT** need.

Think about the things you need to do to achieve each goal – the different steps that must be taken, the time required, your personal attention and your dedication to each step. Develop a simple outline, in the sequence of what must be done first, then next, etc.

It is extremely **important** to **write** your goals and milestones down on paper. **Thinking** about a goal or milestone **does not impart** the same impact to your subconscious. **Your subconscious mind determines your future success, status quo or failure. Thinking, hearing, writing and seeing affects your subconscious differently.**

Think about the <u>rewards</u> of achieving your goals. Assume for a second that your goal was truly <u>noteworthy</u> – to be published in your local paper and/or on TV for all to see. You can be a 'feature story' by a local reporter. For example, it took John two years to learn to fly. Suzie learned to play the piano at the age of 55. Scott learned to speak Chinese in less than two years. Marilyn was recognized three times this past year for her public speaking.

Soak in the satisfaction of finally accomplishing something that was hard for you. Let that feeling come over you and relax you. Allow that happiness to fill you completely. Each time you think about that goal - rekindle that thought of attainment and satisfaction. It will keep you focused. It now becomes your **NO MATTER WHAT** objective. Your fourth **NO MATTER WHAT** decision is to now select one goal and attach as much emotion to it as possible.

In 1930, Watty Piper wrote a children's book called, *The Little Engine That Could.* It focused on a little blue engine that decided to rescue the train when the other engines wouldn't or couldn't. We remember it most for the phrase, 'I think I can, I think I can.'

Thinking is a great start and it is where all of us start – with that thought of what we want or need to achieve. But, when that thought becomes part of us – so much a part of us that we 'feel' we need to achieve it then the focus becomes easier. Setbacks will happen along the way. If you do not learn from them, you allow your poverty mindset to creep back into your life.

You must learn from your mistakes – that is what they are there for. They are free and you should take advantage of them. Ask yourself why, if it did not work. Find out, and do not repeat it. Take another tack and see what happens. The more decisions you make, the better you become. Learning from your mistakes makes the decision process easier over time – and many of those decisions are the ones you need to overcome failure.

Attach emotion to your goal and think of it often. Some experts recommend writing it down and keeping it with you always. Other experts use reminders – sticky notes, colored dots, etc. to remind you randomly through the day to think of your goal and to 'feel' the satisfaction of achieving it - repeatedly. I personally like this method the best. It randomly reminds us of our goal throughout the day.

We rely on others many times to help us. Many times, I decide not to exercise for any reason – time, weather, feeling bad, etc. However, when I have another person working out with me, then the likelihood of not showing up for a workout becomes significantly less. I feel more obligated to do it if someone else is there with me - a shared bonding to achieve a similar goal.

People react differently to required reports – progress reports, project reports, trip reports, budget status, etc. Some people like to let people know what they are doing and some do not.

Write it your own progress report and mail it to yourself. Yes, put it in an envelope, spend the money, and mail it to yourself. This might sound strange, but take some extra effort to ensure success in attaining your number one goal. This degree of dedication is just another tool for you to use.

It works extremely well for some. After several months, you will have a written record of what worked, what did not, who helped you, where you were stuck and for what reason, etc. It will keep you focused, and the writing in longhand will keep you more emotionally involved in achieving the goal. The handwritten record connects directly to your subconscious mind – much more than typing it. If this seems too monumental for your success, create a new e-mail account and e-mail yourself daily on your progress.

Bill Bartmann is one of America's leading authorities on success and failure. Please take the time to get his book, *Billionaire – Secrets to Success*, and read it. Bill Bartmann dropped out of high school, became a gang member, a physical wreck, lacked goals, and was terribly short of self-esteem. He was a 'poster child' from a dysfunctional family growing up poor on the wrong side of town. He was known as a 'troublemaker' by everyone early in his life and an all-around loser.

He changed after an incident in his early life. He has been married for over 30 years and has two daughters. He graduated from college and law school. He practiced law for five years before deciding to become an entrepreneur. He founded several companies in real estate, oil and gas, manufacturing and finance.

Bill Bartmann started from his kitchen table with a $13,000 loan and ended up with a company that produced revenues more than a $1,000,000,000.00 (billion dollars) annually. He was recognized as an innovator, and could take failing businesses and make them profitable. Over the course of his business career, his companies have created jobs for over 10,000 employees. He has earned over $100,000,000.00 (one hundred million dollars) in a year. The list of awards could fill up many more pages. He is typically ranked in the top wealthiest people in America.

Harvard Business School has written a case study based on Bill Bartmann and his management techniques. He is also in the Smithsonian Institute's Museum of American History for his "Visionary Use of Information Technology Which Produces Positive Social, Economic, and Educational Change." Bill Bartmann believes he can achieve anything he sets his mind out to achieve – no exceptions! Bill Bartmann believes in making a 'promise' to do something rather than setting a 'goal' to do something. He believes that a promise has more emotion attached to it and forces us to focus on it differently than just having a goal.

Bill Bartmann was drunk and fell down a flight of stairs when he was seventeen years old. He crushed two vertebrae, ruptured a disc and damaged his spinal cord. He was instantly paralyzed from his waist down. Every test came back the same – he would never regain the use of his lower limbs. He would be confined to a wheelchair and never walk. He had a Significant Emotional Event that changed his decision making.

Some people would accept the diagnosis. Bill did not. He totally rejected the notion that he would never walk again. He 'promised' himself that he would walk out of that hospital – his **NO MATTER WHAT** decision. In the early 1960's, the typical physical rehabilitation was to have the nurse staff release the tension on his traction device for an hour and rub his legs, ankles and feet to improve circulation. He created his own physical rehabilitation – like Morris Goodman, but not employing the positive self-improvement techniques. He would stare at his toes and use his mental and physical strengths to make his toes move. His face would turn red, his veins would bulge out of each side of his head and he would break out in a sweat. He would do this if he could hold it. He would relax a few seconds and begin over – all day long.

The nurses encouraged him to stop and finally had his doctor intervene to make him stop. They did not want him holding out hope for something that was hopeless. The doctor told him to accept his situation for what it was. He was warned by his doctor that if he persisted in his regimen that it would wear him out and prolong his recovery period.

Bill Bartmann was not to be deterred by his doctor, the nurses, or his friends and family. Since the nurses monitored him during the day, he would begin again at night when they could not see what he was doing. He kept his feet covered with a blanket so the hospital staff could not see him trying to wiggle his toes. Eventually, he would exercise all night and sleep during the day.

Two weeks later he managed to wiggle his toes. After he confirmed that he could really wiggle his toes when he wanted to, he contacted the nurse. The nurse agreed he could move his toes when he said he was, and called his doctor. The doctor came in later during his rounds and observed Bill's toes moving. He tested Bill's legs for 'feeling' and found none. He could not explain medically why Bill could control his toes when he was paralyzed, and told him that he would still never walk.

Bill became depressed and then remembered the promise he made to himself – to walk out of that hospital. All hospital tests were in total agreement that his spinal cord injury was irreversible. Spinal cord injuries do not heal themselves! One day, Bill dreamt of a scale, like the one you typically see in a courtroom – Lady Justice. He saw all the evidence the medical profession had declared him an invalid on one side of the scale and his promise on the other side. His promise weighed the same as the medical evidence. He assessed that his promise was equal to the medical evidence. He realized that outcomes are not always based on knowledge or education, but sometimes they are determined by the strength of a person's belief system.

That night he resumed his personal quest to walk out of the hospital. He was successful with his toes – now he would concentrate on his legs. He scooted down to the bottom of the bed and let his feet meet the railing at the foot of the bed. He could not feel his feet touching the railing but he could see them. Bill forced his knees to buckle upward and concentrated on forcing his feet to push him back towards the head of the bed. He kept trying to straighten his legs. He concentrated on his leg muscles for as long and as hard as he could. The nurses would find him at the bottom of the bed and would move him back up to a normal position in his bed every night.

By the third week, he could feel his feet touching the bottom rail of his bed. He could not make his legs straighten, but it was progress. He did not share his progress with the nurses or his doctor. The rest of his recovery happened much faster. Within a few days, he could straighten his legs and push himself off the bottom rail of his bed.

One night he decided that he was going to stand up on the floor. He positioned himself to the edge of his bed and lowered his feet to the floor. He used the bed to steady himself with his feet firmly planted on the floor. After a long while, he slowly stood up while holding on to the bed. He could stand on his own, although his legs were trembling due to loss of muscle strength. He sat back down, rested, and stood up again. Each time he stood, he could stand longer than the time before. Even though he was exhausted from standing, he decided to take a step forward and not hang on to the bed for support. He could walk very slowly in a stiff-kneed motion, sliding one foot forward at a time.

Bill Bartmann got back to his bed and pressed the nurse's call button. He then turned around and shuffled back to the middle of the room away from the bed. The nurses entered the room quickly and were startled by someone standing in the middle of a dark room. They let out a scream and that brought more nurses to his room. After five months of being bedridden, he could stand on his own. Two weeks later Bill Bartmann walked out of the hospital under his own power.

Summary

Your 4th **NO MATTER WHAT** decision is to select a goal and attach emotion to it.

- We live every day of our life in our Poverty Industrial Complex or our Prosperity Industrial Complex.
- The difference between living in the Poverty Industrial Complex and the Prosperity Industrial Complex is the decisions we make daily in our lives.
- Poverty and Prosperity are a mindset – not a financial status.
- **Guideline #6:** Change your mindset to change your lifestyle.
- Your mindset is programmed since birth by your family, friends and the experiences you have in life.
- The average eighteen-year-old has been told NO at least 80,000 times in his life.

- Many of us are programmed to accept life as it is dealt to us.

- Negativity programs our subconscious mind to be minimal – to keep us from growing.

- **Guideline #7:** Don't accept goals others set for you or you will never disappoint them.

- 80% of what we see, hear and read is negative programming.

- **Guideline #8:** Recognize negativity for what it is.

- **Guideline #9:** Recognize negativity in your life is not benefitting you.

- **Guideline #10:** You must leave your comfort zone to improve your life.

- **Guideline #11:** Do not allow negativity to affect you emotionally.

- **Guideline #12:** Program positivity into your life daily.

- **Guideline #13:** Eliminate what you say to others with a negative tone.

- **Guideline #14:** Make positive responses every day for at least the next 21 days.

- **Guideline #15:** If you cannot change your friends, you probably need to change your friends.

No Matter What You Can Do It

- **Guideline #16:** You cannot afford to maintain relationships with negative or disempowering friends if you want to improve your life.

- **Guideline #17:** Keep a positive attitude.

- Attitude determines so many things in your life.

- **Guideline #18:** Visualize your goal achievement – how it makes you feel to have achieved your goal.

- Visualizing goals help keep you focused.

- **Guideline #19:** Add emotion to your decisions by visualizing your goals.

- **Guideline #20:** Know what it takes to achieve your goal – each step along the way – outline each in the sequence of what needs to be done next.

- **Guideline #21:** Write your goals in longhand. It imparts more emotional attachment to your subconscious mind.

- **Guideline #22:** Take advantage of thinking, hearing, seeing and writing your goals because each affects your subconscious mind differently.

- Your subconscious mind determines your success, your failure and/or your status quo.

- **Guideline #23:** Convert your thinking processes to feeling so that your goals are easier to achieve.

- **Guideline #24:** Learn from your mistakes – understand why you failed.

- **Guideline #25:** Attach emotions to your goals and think of them often.

- **Guideline #26:** Use reminders to constantly alert you to your goal. Make them evoke emotion in you when you see them.

- The more aligned emotionally you are with your goal the higher the probability of success.

- **Guideline #27:** Ensure your goals are realistic.

- **Guideline #28:** Take advantage of assistance from others to help you achieve your goals.

- **Guideline #29:** Do the Report Exercise monthly. Look for trends after six months to help you improve.

- **Guideline #30:** Make a promise rather than a goal if you want to add more emotion to it.

- **Guideline #31:** Don't accept situations for what they are.

- Outcomes are not always based on knowledge and education, but sometimes by the strength of a person's belief system.

"Promises Are More Powerful Than Goals." Bill Bartmann

No Matter What You Can Do It

"True success is achieving YOUR goal – not one set by someone else." Bill Bartmann

"Imagination is more important than knowledge." Albert Einstein

"Set you mind and keep it on the higher things." Ephesians 2:7

Psycho-Cybernetics

Maxwell Maltz, M.D., F.I.C.S. wrote, *Psycho-Cybernetics* in 1960. Dr. Maltz, a cosmetic surgeon, began studying 'self-image psychology' in the 1950s based on the results of his patients' recoveries. When ugliness was removed, it took about 21 days for the patient to rise in self-esteem and self-confidence – but this did not happen to all his patients. Even though some were literally 'perfect' compared to what they were before surgery, they still felt feelings of inferiority – they viewed the surgery as a failure – they retained the ugliness they had before surgery, even though their disfigurement was totally removed and looked as normal as any other person. **Everyone has a self-image of himself or herself. The key to truly being successful in life is to change your self-image.**

Dr. Maltz found that it took a minimum of <u>21 days</u> for his patients to <u>change</u> their <u>self-image</u> of themselves on the average.

He was very careful to distinguish between the terms success and successful. Everyone should attempt to be successful – that is, acquiring satisfaction, fulfillment and happiness rather than acquiring prestige symbols.

Many of us are <u>programmed</u> early in life to be <u>failures</u>. We might be told that we <u>can't</u> spell, <u>can't</u> sell, <u>can't</u> talk in public, or <u>can't</u> solve a math problem, etc. If you tell yourself, *"I am a failure."* – you are reinforcing your belief system into your subconscious mind. It is better to tell yourself, *"I failed a test."* - that is an <u>accurate</u> and <u>factual</u> <u>statement</u>. Stating a fact is different from believing that you are a failure since you failed. These are two different things and they are integrated into your psyche differently.

Today you hear that you must become what you want to become first - before you become it. You currently have a baseline – <u>an internal psychological baseline</u> – of who you are and what you can do. You must change your internal psychological baseline to who you want to become before you can achieve it.

Your self-image is the basis of your self-esteem. It is what you trust about yourself and what you truly believe. It is a reasonable approximation of who you are – no more, no less. Do you know the difference between <u>self-confidence</u> and <u>self-esteem</u>? It is mandatory to know the difference. You might want to check the dictionary. One might lack self-esteem and exude self-confidence.

Dr. Maltz discovered that your subconscious mind is not a 'mind' per se, but a <u>mechanism</u> – a goal-striving 'servo-mechanism' consisting of your brain and your nervous system that is used and directed by your subconscious mind. Your subconscious mind is awake <u>24 hours a day</u> – it does not rest. **It guides you in all you do**. Your conscious mind can <u>direct</u> and <u>change</u> the <u>baseline</u> of your subconscious mind.

Give yourself a <u>positive goal</u> and your subconscious will function positively and will do all it can to achieve your positive goal. Give yourself a <u>negative goal</u> and your subconscious will function negatively and will do all it can to achieve your negative goal. Therefore, the statement, *"I'm a failure."* is so much more powerful than saying, *"I failed that test."* **"I'm a failure." drives your subconscious mind to become a failure.**

Your subconscious operates in two basic modes –**The first mode is where the goal is <u>known</u> and the <u>objective</u> is to <u>reach</u> that goal. The second mode is where the goal is <u>not known</u> and the objective is to discover <u>how</u> to reach that goal.**

Assume you have a goal and you know 'how' to achieve it. Your subconscious mind adjusts keep you directed or focused on achieving your goal. When you drive a car, your goal is to stay in the lane you are driving in - unless you want to change lanes. As you drive in that lane, you make minor adjustments left or right to keep you in that lane. These left and right corrections are **negative feedback loops** – failures that have been recognized and corrections made to counter each failure. These negative feedback loops are like the adjustments your subconscious mind makes to help you achieve your goal. It has a target, it knows how to get there, and it will keep you moving in that direction. These are 'successful' responses to achieving your goal.

Successful responses are remembered in your subconscious mind for future use. Your subconscious mind remembers successful actions and over time failures are minimized to a point that they seem like they almost did not happen to you. The sheer quantity of positive experiences far outweighs your earlier negative experiences. It will remember how you failed and it will prevent you from doing the same in the future. **Over time, the successful actions guide you as if it were a habit.**

Failure is necessary for your life to learn. Accept failure for what it is – a <u>temporary deviation</u> from your destination/goal. Some people say, 'things happen for a reason'. I believe that also. They become life's biggest learning opportunities. Turn them into negative feedback loops for your personal success.

In the second mode, your brain attempts to find the target when it is not known – your subconscious mind must approximate that target based on the information it has acquired over time. Your subconscious mind will search its banks of data for those targets that meet the criteria described in your original problem. Remember the last time you knew someone's name but could not remember it at that moment. You might say to yourself – I think his name starts with an 'S' - or something like that. You think and cannot dig it out of your brain. However, go on to something else and your subconscious mind will dredge it out when you are not expecting it.

Dr. Maltz tells us that an unhappy, failure type personality cannot develop a new self-image by pure will power or by arbitrarily deciding to do it. There must be some over-riding reason or justification for deciding that the old_'you' is in error and must – must be changed. In sensing a need to change for the better – a person must see or realize the truth about him or herself. Therefore, to change your subconscious mind you must have a success mechanism that has a goal that is achievable now or in potential form. Your subconscious mind will steer you by what it already knows or by discovering something already in existence.

Continue to always think in terms of the result. Your subconscious mind will get you there. Do not be afraid of making mistakes – realize them for what they are – **negative feedback loops** that will automatically correct you back onto your course – towards your target.

No Matter What You Can Do It

Napoleon said, *"Imagination rules the world."* Dr. Maltz believes that you always act, feel and perform in accordance with what you imagine **to be true** about yourself or your environment. Your imagination sets your goal picture and then your automatic subconscious mechanism works to accomplish it. **You act or fail to act, not because of will, but because of your imagination.**

Your subconscious mind governs your nervous system. It can be proved when people are under hypnosis. Tell them that they touched something hot or cold and the body's internal systems will react accordingly. Your nervous system cannot tell the difference between an imagined experience and a real experience. It reacts automatically to the information you think or imagine to be true.

Many tests have been done over the years proving that imagining yourself achieving your goal works. One of the best examples are given in Dr. Maltz' book involves a successful salesman. He imagined every situation in which he can present his sale and every objection that can be raised. He worked out a solution for each objection and knew how to counter each objection before it ever arose. By imagining the situations and potential objections, the salesman built confidence and success. It is very like going in for a job interview. Be prepared for that inevitable question – *"Tell me a little about yourself."* If you have already rehearsed that question before the interview, you can answer it in a relaxed manner and can stop at any point in time and address any aspect with further clarity.

This process works today in sports. Teams practice and practice, and when the time comes, they execute, and the ball goes exactly where it was intended. The subconscious mind was trained so well that it controlled the muscles correctly to make the goal attainable.

Your self-image is built on your imagination of yourself. If you imagine defeat, then you are defeated. If you imagine success, then you will be successful. It takes a minimum of 21 days and lots of practice to change your negative self-image. Dr. Maltz suggests that you actively take some time each day and exercise your imagination.

Dr. Lee Pulos, a registered psychologist, author, entrepreneur, and master educator has made a study of the human mind. Dr. Pulos tells us that at birth humans have 120,000,000,000 (one hundred twenty billion) glial cells - active neurons in our brain. As you develop and grow older, unused neurons become dormant. By the time you get to your adult years, the number of active neurons is around 10,000,000,000 (ten billion). These neurons are used for your conscious and subconscious thought processes. Through his research and study, Dr. Pulos revealed that in one second of time your conscious mind uses about 2,000 active neurons while your subconscious mind uses 4,000,000,000 (four billion). This means that every second of your life your conscious mind uses 2,000 active neurons to make conscious decisions and your subconscious mind uses 4,000,000,000 (four billion) active neurons to make subconscious decisions. (Note: Many of those neurons are used by your subconscious mind for your normal body processes – breathing, heartbeat, etc.) For everyone active neuron involved in your active decision process, there are 2,000,000 (two million) active neurons operating the decision processes in your subconscious mind. **Your subconscious mind has control of everything you do.**

Your conscious mind can control your subconscious mind if you program it correctly. I recently listened to Vince Poscente, a motivational expert and Olympic athlete, talk about Dr. Pulos' work. He equated it to an ant riding on the back of an elephant. The ant is your conscious thought process and the elephant is your subconscious thought process. You may have a goal to go west, but if the elephant is going east, you will never reach your goal. You may be facing west and not actually travel in that direction. Your overall progress is the reverse – and you do not even know it. Vince goes into detail about these processes in his book, *The Ant and the Elephant.*

Think about succeeding in accomplishing your big goal. Visualize yourself on TV or on the movie screen. Make it as vivid and detailed as possible. By doing this you will build images of success in your subconscious mind. Your subconscious mind cannot tell real from imagined; and, if you can stuff it full of descriptive images of your success, then, over time your subconscious mind will believe you are successful and will help you accomplish your goals. Build memories daily of your personal success as you reach one goal after another. Become that person you want to become. Over time, you will find yourself becoming that person – not by trying, but literally without trying.

Dr. Maltz estimates that 95% of people have feelings of inferiority to some degree that inhibit their success and happiness. Feelings of inferiority originate not from the <u>actual</u> events you experience in your life, but from your <u>conclusions</u> about them. It is the old *"I'm a failure"* versus *"I failed that test"* syndrome. **When you judge yourself against someone else's ability, then you fail yourself.**

There are many **NO MATTER WHAT** examples of successful athletes achieving record-setting performances. Pick a sport – there are many of them. Coaches and mentors inspire their athletes to become better than they could have become by themselves. I mentioned Vince Poscente earlier and his book, *The Ant and the Elephant*. Unlike most superstar athletes, Vince went from recreational skier to the Olympic finals in speed skiing <u>in less than four years</u>. Vince never participated in speed skiing prior to his decision to become the best in the world. He accomplished his goal of making it to the Olympic finals through practice and mind control. A speed skier goes faster down a mountain slope than a person does falling from an airplane. Vince holds the Canadian world record in speed skiing at 216.7 km/hr.

Vince tells his story of wanting to be an Olympic athlete very early in his life. He and another friend decided they would become Olympic finalists in the luge. Luge is either a one or two-person sled. The competitive events are raced against time. The faster person/team wins.

The problem was that neither of them had ever done the luge before. As they progressed in training for this event, they proved their inability and lack of skill and were told to 'give it up.' Vince took the advice seriously and he and his friend parted company. Several years later, the Olympics were held in Calgary, Canada and Vince bought a ticket and watched all the athletes enter the stadium on the first day of the Games. Canada, being the host country, entered the stadium last. Vince remembers vividly seeing his former 'luge partner' of several years earlier, marching in with the Canadian National Olympic team – as a competitor in the luge event. Vince thought to himself – *"Why am I here holding a ticket and my friend qualified for the Olympics?"*

It was that instant that Vince made up his mind to become an Olympic athlete – his **NO MATTER WHAT** decision. He had a natural ability in skiing and felt that this area would be his most probable route to the Olympics. The next Olympics were scheduled for Albertville, France. The host country, France, selected speed skiing as an event. Vince decided that he would win this event – it was another **NO MATTER WHAT** decision.

Vince had no experience going down a slope over 100 miles/hour, but it was not going to stop him! As he describes the event, the skier is perched at the top of a slope and the timer announces a start to the skier. The skier has 60 seconds to begin his descent. The slope is between 40 and 45 degrees downward. The skier attains a speed more than 60 miles/hour in three seconds. In eight seconds, he is going as fast as a person falls through the air when he exits an airplane without a parachute – 125 miles/hour. The skier's speed is measured at the end of the course.

This is not an event in which you can go anywhere and practice. Vince decided to look at all options – to fully educate himself in every possible area to separate himself from his competition. Vince Poscente has a motto – **Do What Your Competition Will Not Do!**

He preaches this at his motivational seminars. Vince began studying laminar flow and mind control – doing what his competition would not do. He called a major aircraft manufacturer and asked if he could use their wind tunnel to practice his speed skiing. He thought if he could feel the drag on his body in different orientations he would be able to minimize the drag on his body going downhill and go faster than his competition. The aircraft manufacturer was certainly willing to help, but the wind tunnel cost $1,000.00/hour. Vince was on a budget and it did not include this expense.

Vince had to get creative to be competitive – <u>doing what his competitors would not do.</u> How do you make your own wind tunnel? He strapped himself to the roof of a friend's car and they took off driving down the highway. He also developed the mental discipline to focus on his goal and become good enough to qualify for the World and Olympic qualifying events. As part of his mental focus, he had to clarify his goal. **Your goal must be 'crystal clear'.**

Not only that, you must have an **emotional relationship with your goal**. If it does not give you a 'buzz', it is not defined well enough. Every time you think of your goal – the big "WHY" – you must have some level of energy pulse through your body. He used 'gold dots' to remind him of his goal. He placed them everywhere – even when he traveled. He would have them in his wallet, on his mirror, in his car, around his home – literally scattered about his environment. Every time he saw his 'gold dot', the thrill of winning the speed skiing event would kick in.

I mentioned the ant and the elephant concept earlier. The conscious mind sees the gold dot and imparts an imaginary, yet 'real feeling' to the subconscious mind. Thus, you align your conscious thought process with your subconscious thought process. You now have the ant and the elephant both going in the same direction - towards your goal. Vince found studying mind control, motivation, self-improvement to be vital in his preparation to earn a qualifying berth in the Olympics and to make it to the finals. Vince Poscente summarizes the lessons he learned through his experience in his book, *Invinceable Principles – Essential Tools for Life Mastery*.

Summary:

- Everyone has a self-image of himself or herself.
- The key to success in life is to change your self-image.
- You can re-enforce failure into your subconscious mind just by saying, "I am a failure."
- **Guideline #32:** Don't say, "I am a failure." Say, "I failed that exam or test."
- You must believe you are the new person you want to become before you can become him or her.
- Your self-image is the basis of your self-esteem. It is what you trust about yourself.
- Your subconscious mind operates 24 hours a day.
- Your subconscious mind guides you in everything you do.

- Your conscious mind can guide and control your subconscious mind.

- Your subconscious mind works when you know your goal and how to achieve it.

- Your subconscious mind also works when you know your goal and don't know how to achieve it.

- **Guideline #33:** Ask yourself, "How do I do it" questions, when you don't know how to achieve your goal. Let your subconscious figure it out for you.

- Negative feedback loops are corrections to errors – they adjust you back onto the course.

- **Guideline #34:** Overload your subconscious mind with endless thoughts of success to minimize or erase the negative programming you already have.

- Failure is necessary to learn.

- Willpower cannot change your self-image.

- There must be an overriding reason to change the old you – or, it will never happen. The subconscious must see the reason – know why it needs to change.

- **Guideline #35:** Always think in terms of the successful result.

- We act or fail to act because of our imagination – what we imagine to be true.

- Your subconscious cannot tell the difference between real and imagined.

- Imagine defeat and you will be defeated. Imagine failure and you will fail.

- Image success and you will be successful.

- It takes a minimum of 21 days to change your self-image.

- **Guideline #36:** Exercise your imagination daily.

- Your subconscious controls you. Control your subconscious to take control of your future.

- **Guideline #37:** Ensure your images of your success are as vivid and detailed as possible.

- **Guideline #38:** Ensure your goals are crystal clear.

- **Guideline #39:** Build memories daily of the success you will become.

- Feelings of inferiority are not based on actual events, but on your perceptions of what happened.

- **Guideline #40:** Don't judge yourself against others' abilities.

- Do what your competition will not do.

- If you don't have an emotional buzz when you think about your goals, then they aren't defined well enough.

- **Guideline #41:** Align your conscious and subconscious through multiple iterations of your success.

"All that we are is the result of what we have thought. The mind is everything. What we think, we become." Buddha

Mentoring

The Social Security Administration tracks many interesting statistics throughout our working lives. One that I found literally amazing is that out of 100 people working from age 20 till age 65 – that's 45 years of working at least 40 hours a week for most of us - the record shows:

- Five are still working at age 65.
- Twenty-eight didn't make it that far – they died before reaching age 65. Sixty-two are 'dead broke', that is, they are sustaining themselves below the poverty level and are not working for a variety of reasons – sickness, disability, etc.
- That's 95 out of 100.
- The other five are composed of one person who is rich and the other four are independently wealthy.
- **5% made it to financial freedom and 95% failed.**

No Matter What You Can Do It

As I said earlier, I thought these facts were <u>literally amazing</u>! You have heard of the 'haves' and the 'have not's. Breaking it down statistically, it appears that 5% of us belong to the 'haves' and 95% of us belong to the 'have not's. It is scary to think that you have a <u>95%</u> chance of failure in one of the greatest countries our world has ever seen. Do you want to know something very interesting – the mere fact that you are reading this book means that you, yes you, can change the odds in your favor. Like everything else in life, it does not come easy. Yet, many of you are willing to invest years of your time and many, many dollars of your hard-earned money to get a college degree – and maybe even another advanced college degree. **Does that <u>guarantee</u> you that you will belong to that financially independent 5% club? NO! It does not.**

Many of you spend your time and money making yourselves more valuable to others. Many of you do not invest any comparable time and money on your own 'future self'.

You have already invested time and money in my *No Matter What* book. Please make another **NO MATTER WHAT** decision – to continue your self-improvement after you have completed reading it.

I have listened to Dave Ramsey, a well-known financial guidance expert, in person and on the radio, talk about personal financial management – basically living within your means. He says, "**If you live like nobody else, you can live like nobody else**." You take the time now to plant those seeds of financial discipline, and they will bring you a harvest so you can live like the 5% well before you are 65 years of age.

My mentor, Myron Golden, tells me that there is a simple two-sentence formula for achieving wealth during our lives. **If you want to be rich – find out what the rich people are doing and do those things. Find out what the poor people are doing and don't do those things.**

I mentioned that I have a mentor. All of you should have a mentor – whether you are at work or home. You need to network with the 'rich and famous.' I am not talking about the celebrities that you too often see in the movies, on TV and read about in the newspapers. I am talking about the successful people at work and in your community - those people you have access to daily.

Realistically your mentor should be in your sphere of influence – in other words – he or she should be accessible to you. Ask your potential mentor if he or she ever had a mentor. At least, open a conversation to see where it might lead.

Thomas J. Stanley and William D. Danko, in their book, *The Millionaire Next Door*, reinforce what Dave Ramsey has been telling us daily. Most the millionaires are not the glitzy, big-spending tycoons that the media shows us. But, they are just like you and me. In many cases, they did not inherit their wealth or have advanced degrees. They worked hard – as most of us do every day. They lived within their means and saved – as Dave Ramsey tells us to do.

I define a millionaire as a person who nets a million dollars a year in compensation, investment dividends or other cash flow into their active accounts – not equity tied up in houses or their 401K or equivalent accounts. Are they that hard to find?

If I want financial freedom, as many of us want, then there must be some mental picture of how you would handle your accounts.

- Would you tithe?
- Would you invest?
- Would you give to charities?
- Would you set up a legacy for your children and grandchildren?
- Would you become debt free before embarking on your fantasy vacation or buying your dream home with cash?

Does that mean if I follow Dave Ramsey's advice, you will be rich? No, but it does mean you might not be dead broke at age 65. One day a caller asked Dave what his success record was for those who took his advice. He said 'probably close to 90% of those who started with written budgets gave up after a very short time. About ten percent actually had the discipline to stick it out and pull themselves out of debt.' That's a bit better than the Social Security Administration's <u>95%</u> failure rate. **Writing it down it makes it easier for you to accomplish your goals. A budget is another tool to get you to financial freedom.**

Why do you still fail when you know what to do? When you have a medical problem, you go to a medical doctor to have it identified and corrected. When you have a problem with your car, you take it to a mechanic and find out what's wrong and decide to correct it or not. When you have a legal problem, you go to a lawyer and find out what remedy you might have. However, when most of you have financial problems, you do not go to financial specialists to find out what your problem is and what options are available to fix them.

Most of us typically go to our family or friends – those most likely to end up in the 95% group at the end of their lives. Why do you trust someone who is not wealthy, not making successful money decisions daily to guide you in your journey to a better financial life?

David Chilton is the author of the book, *The Wealthy Barber*, - *Everyone's Commonsense Guide to Becoming Financially Independent*. I liked this book because of the style in which it is written – almost like a novel. It is an easy read – something that most of us could read within a week without spending hours and hours reading. It is a 'commonsense guide' that is easy to follow both in learning and doing. While I am plugging books that I have read, let me also plug Dave Ramsey's *Financial Peace University,* plus several other books he has written on financial understanding and planning.

If you do not ask your brother-in-law or uncle for financial advice and you begin to look at those things rich people do and those things poor people do – **can you become financially independent? The answer is still NO! Why?** It is not only knowing and planning what to do. **It is the execution!**

Look at any major sporting event – baseball, football, basketball, etc. When it comes time for the 'must win', each team knows their strengths and weaknesses and the other teams' strengths and weaknesses. They know their game plans and have back-ups for this and that contingency. One team wins and one team loses. It is in the execution. This example might be a bit of overkill, but it underscores the importance of having a plan and sticking with it.

The military will tell you that a war plan does not survive past the first bullet fired. Plans change to meet the battlefield conditions. Assume that you now know what you want. Now a plan must be drafted on 'how' to get there. Myron Golden tells us that you need to know what the rich people do and what the poor people do and follow one group and do not follow the other. Here is where things start getting a bit tougher for most of us.

No Matter What You Can Do It

I mentioned two teams competing against each other to attain a 'must win' for their side. What if you had a team that was working with you for a common goal of success? They are out there and they need you just as much as you need them. Similarly, having another person to work out with or to share in the burden of some hardship or dreadful task – it is easier when you have help. You need someone to work with you – you need a network. You need a network of successful people – at least, people more successful than you to get started. You need the **Brotherhood of Prosperity.**

When you know someone, you will find out that they know someone, and that person knows someone. You would not pass up that connection if you were trying to get that perfect job. However, for some reason, you do not use that network for your 'future self'. The Brotherhood of Prosperity is composed of successful entrepreneurs. They have succeeded and want to share their lessons learned with you. Some are available to you in person – in your work or social environment. Some are available to you through books, CDs, DVDs and the Internet. They are out there and they want to help you.

It is a lot easier to have someone on the inside aware of what your needs and willing to help you. They can help pull you into a better position, rather than you fighting by yourself, pushing against the obstacles, barriers and constraints that you cannot see.

[handwritten margin note: Why network?]

Look around at the people you would consider successful. People generally like to talk about themselves. Ask some of them for a few minutes of their time – tell them that you would like to know how they achieved success in their lives. After talking to several of them, you should see a common thread – something that is similar in each story. You might even find one of them telling you that if you want to talk further in the future to let them know. Now you are on the cusp of having a personal network. There is still a long way to go, but having a line drawn in the sand will help you begin that journey. You know what you want – you will recognize it when you get there. You know some people to ask for guidance when it is needed. You have the beginning of a plan that will point you in the right direction.

A Message to Garcia

Elbert Hubbard - December 1, 1913

Foreword

This literary trifle, *A Message to Garcia*, was written one evening after supper, in a single hour. It was on the 22nd of February 1899, Washington's Birthday: we were just going to press with the *March Philistine*.

No Matter What You Can Do It

The thing leaped hot from my heart, written after a trying day when I had been endeavoring to train some rather delinquent villagers to abjure the comatose state and get radioactive.

The immediate suggestion, though, came from a little argument over the teacups, when my boy, Bert, suggested that Rowan was the real hero of the Cuban War. Rowan had gone alone and done the thing - carried the message to Garcia.

It came to me like a flash! Yes, the boy is right, the hero is the man who does his work - who carries the message to Garcia. I got up from the table and wrote *A Message to Garcia*. I thought so little of it that we ran it in the Magazine without a heading. The edition went out, and soon orders began to come for extra copies of the *March Philistine*, a dozen, fifty, a hundred, and when the American News Company ordered a thousand, I asked one of my helpers which article it was that stirred up the cosmic dust. *"It's the stuff about Garcia,"* he said.

The next day a telegram came from George H. Daniels, of the New York Central Railroad, thus, "Give price on one hundred thousand Rowan article in pamphlet form - Empire State Express advertisement on back - also how soon can ship."

I replied giving a price, and stated we could supply the pamphlets in two years. Our facilities were small and a hundred thousand booklets looked like an awful undertaking.

No Matter What You Can Do It

The result was that I gave Mr. Daniels permission to reprint the article in his own way. He issued it in booklet form in editions of half a million. Two or three of these half-million lots were sent out by Mr. Daniels, and, in addition, the article was reprinted in over two hundred magazines and newspapers. It has been translated into all written languages.

At the time, Mr. Daniels was distributing *A Message to Garcia*, Prince Hilakoff, Director of Russian Railways, was in this country. He was the guest of the New York Central and made a tour of the country under the personal direction of Mr. Daniels. The Prince saw the little book and was interested in it, more because Mr. Daniels was putting it out in big numbers, probably than otherwise. In any event, when he got home he had the matter translated into Russian and a copy of the booklet given to every railroad employee in Russia.

Other countries then took it up, and from Russia it passed into Germany, France, Spain, Turkey, Hindustan and China. During the war between Russia and Japan, every Russian soldier who went to the front was given a copy of *A Message to Garcia*. The Japanese, finding the booklets in possession of the Russian prisoners, concluded it must be a good thing, and accordingly translated it into Japanese.

And on an order of the Mikado, a copy was given to every man in the employ of the Japanese Government, soldier or civilian.

No Matter What You Can Do It

memorandum for me concerning the life of Correggio." Will the clerk quietly say, *"Yes, sir,"* and go do the task?

On your life, he will not. He will look at you out of a fishy eye and ask one or more of the following questions: Who was he? Which encyclopedia? Where is the encyclopedia? Was I hired for that? Don't you mean Bismarck? What's the matter with Charlie doing it? Is he dead? Is there any hurry? Sha'n't I bring you the book and let you look it up yourself? What do you want to know for?

And I will lay you ten to one that after you have answered the questions, and explained how to find the information, and why you want it, the clerk will go off and get one of the other clerks to help him try to find Correggio - and then come back and tell you there is no such man. Of course, I may lose my bet, but according to the Law of Average, I will not.

Now, if you are wise, you will not bother to explain to your "assistant" that Correggio is indexed under the C's, not in the K's, but you will smile very sweetly and say, "Never mind," and go look it up yourself. And this incapacity for independent action, this moral stupidity, this infirmity of the will, this unwillingness to cheerfully catch hold and lift - these are the things that put pure Socialism so far into the future. If men will not act for themselves, what will they do when the benefit of their effort is for all?

No Matter What You Can Do It

A first mate with knotted club seems necessary; and the dread of getting "the bounce." Saturday night holds many a worker to his place. Advertise for a stenographer, and nine out of ten who apply can neither spell nor punctuate - and do not think it necessary to.

Can such a one write a letter to Garcia? *"You see that bookkeeper,"* said the foreman to me in a large factory. Yes, what about him?" *"Well he's a fine accountant, but if I'd send him up town on an errand, he might accomplish the errand all right, and on the other hand, might stop at four saloons on the way, and when he got to Main Street would forget what he had been sent for."* Can such a man be entrusted to carry a message to Garcia?

We have recently been hearing much maudlin sympathy expressed for the "downtrodden denizens of the sweat-shop" and the "homeless wanderer searching for honest employment," and with it all often go many hard words for the men in power.

Nothing is said about the employer who grows old before his time in a vain attempt to get frowsy ne'er-do-wells to do intelligent work; and his long, patient striving after "help" that does nothing but loaf when his back is turned.

In every store and factory, there is a constant weeding-out process going on. The employer is constantly sending away "help" that have shown their incapacity to further the interests of the business, and others are being taken on. No matter how good times are, this sorting continues: only, if times are hard and work is scarce, the sorting is done finer - but out and forever out the incompetent and unworthy go. It is the survival of the fittest. Self-interest prompts every employer to keep the best - those who can carry a message to Garcia.

I know one man of brilliant parts who has not the ability to manage a business of his own, and yet who is absolutely worthless to anyone else because he carries with him constantly the insane suspicion that his employer is oppressing, or intending to oppress him. He cannot give orders, and he will not receive them. Should a message be given him to take to Garcia, his answer would probably be, *"Take it yourself!"*

Tonight, this man walks the streets looking for work, the wind whistling through his threadbare coat. No one who knows him dares employ him, for he is a regular firebrand of discontent. He is impervious to reason, and the only thing that can impress him is the toe of a thick-soled Number Nine boot.

Of course, I know that one so morally deformed is no less to be pitied than a physical cripple; but in our pitying, let us drop a tear, too, for the men who are striving to carry on a great enterprise, whose working hours are not limited by the whistle, and whose hair is fast turning white through the struggle to hold in line dowdy indifference, slipshod imbecility, and the heartless ingratitude which, but for their enterprise, would be both hungry and homeless.

Have I put the matter too strongly? Possibly I have; but when all the world has gone a-slumming, I wish to speak a word of sympathy for the man who succeeds - the man who, against great odds, has directed the efforts of others, and having succeeded, finds there's nothing in it: nothing but bare board and clothes. I have carried a dinner pail and worked for day's wages, and I have also been an employer of labor, and I know there is something to be said on both sides.

There is no excellence, per se, in poverty; rags are no recommendation, and all employers are not rapacious and high-handed, any more than all poor men are virtuous. My heart goes out to the man who does his work when the "boss" is away, as well as when he is at home. And the man who, when given a letter for Garcia, quietly takes the missive, without asking any idiotic questions, and with no lurking intention of chucking it into the nearest sewer, or of doing aught else but deliver it, never gets "laid off" nor must go on a strike for higher wages.

Civilization is one long anxious search for just such individuals. Anything such a man asks shall be granted. He is wanted in every city, town and village - in every office, shop, store and factory. The world cries out for such: he is needed and needed badly - the man who can "Carry a Message to Garcia."

No Matter What You Can Do It

Andrew Summers Rowen was a graduate of West Point in 1881. In 1898, the United States was preparing to invade Cuba. The United States wanted to contact the leader of the Cuban insurgents, General Calixto Garcia e Iniguez. General Garcia had been fighting for Cuban independence from Spain since the Ten Years' War of 1868-1878. He had sought the help of the United States. It was critical that both General Garcia and the United States Army knew who was going to attack where to minimize 'friendly' casualties. It was a **NO MATTER WHAT** decision that was made by President McKinley. That information must be known before the United States committed to helping the Cuban resistance.

Elbert Hubbard died when the RMS Lusitania was sunk in 1915. *A Message to Garcia* was made into a motion picture (silent film) in 1916 by Thomas A. Edison, Inc. The first 'talkie' was made in 1936 by Twentieth Century Fox.

In the last chapter, I noted that Vince Poscente's motto is to do what your competitor will not do. Lieutenant Rowan did what others would not think of doing. He knew what needed to be done when the President of the United States gave him a task. What drove his **NO MATTER WHAT** programming to accomplish this mission in a timely manner will never be known. However, there is the desire to accomplish the mission that most military men have ingrained in them through training – and that is the fear of failure. Maybe both drove him to achieve his **NO MATTER WHAT** decision to deliver a message to Garcia.

Summary:

Your 5th **NO MATTER WHAT** decision: Continue your self-improvement after you complete this book.

- 95 out of 100 are not ready for retirement when they turn 65 years old.
- Most of us concentrate of adding our value to their companies – not to our futures.
- **Guideline #42:** Invest in yourself first.
- **Guideline #43:** Live within your means.
- **Guideline #44:** Plant seeds of financial discipline.
- **Guideline #45:** Plant seeds of success.
- **Guideline #46:** Find out what rich people do to be ready for retirement. Do the same.
- **Guideline #47:** Find out what poor people do to be in dire straits for retirement. Avoid every one of these actions.
- **Guideline #48:** Get a mentor.
- **Guideline #49:** Start/Join a success network in your community.

- **Guideline #50:** Plan, on paper, how to spend a million dollars a year on a continual basis.
- **Guideline #51:** Invest, Tithe, Give to Charity.
- **Guideline #52:** Set up a legacy for your family.
- **Guideline #53:** Become debt free.
- **Guideline #54:** Have a written budget.
- Writing it down makes it easier to happen – To Do List, Milestones, Goals, Budget, etc.
- **Guideline # 55:** Accomplish the first milestone on your journey to your earliest goal.
- Budgeting is a tool everyone should use regularly.
- **Guideline #56:** Don't accept advice from non-financial 'experts'. Make sure they have good track records in the areas of financial planning that you need.
- **Guideline #57:** Read two books on financial planning within the next two months.
- **Guideline #58:** Know, plan and execute the actions needed to accomplish your first milestone.
- **Guideline #59:** Find a Brotherhood of Prosperity in your community.
- **Guideline #60:** Start actively participating in at least one social network.

No Matter What You Can Do It

- **Guideline #61:** Invest in yourself. Buy or borrow CDs, book, DVDs. Attend a seminar. Research the Internet for articles and videos on success, prosperity and goal setting.
- **Guideline #62:** Talk to five successful people about their success. Do one a month for the next five months.
- **Guideline #63:** Act promptly and concentrate your energies on accomplishing your milestones.

"The tragedy of life is not that it ends so soon, but that we wait so long to begin it!" W. M. Lewis

"We cannot become what we need to be by remaining what we are." Max DePree

"Whatever doesn't kill you makes you stronger." Friedrich Nietzsche

"Set your mind on things above." Colossians 3:2

Self-Awareness

I discussed the need to change your mindset to become the person you need to be -- to handle the 'new' you in your future. Your subconscious mind is the key to making that change. **Your subconscious mind only understands commands in the present tense**. <u>It does not understand the future</u>. It can re-enforce negativity as well as positivity.

Who are you? How do you define yourself? Do you know your constraints and boundaries? Do you know your comfort zone? How much negativity is there in your life? These are just a few of the questions you need to ask yourself to begin your self-awareness phase. Start first with your self-esteem. It is the key to building a positive you for the future.

Maybe because every time you get evaluated in life the system always focuses on the '<u>negatives</u>' or '<u>weaknesses</u>' in your performance. In the government, military and civilian workplaces, an appraisal system is usually set up to reward performance. However, many times it includes a listing of what you need to improve. At some point in your performance assessment, there is always 'room for improvement' or some other catch-all phrase used to describe where one is weak compared to your boss' expectations.

That might be fine for assessing your working environment, but negativity breeds further negativity. If you want to see the real you, then you should look at your strengths instead of your weaknesses in your self-assessment. All of you have talent – something that you are born with that gives you an edge over others when compared one to one. It is a natural ability to do something. A talent could be good hand-eye coordination. That is why some people can throw a ball much more accurately than others.

Skills do not come with birth; however, they can be developed and honed with practice. Start with your talent and continue to improve upon it. Add the skills, knowledge and practice necessary to grow your positive image. **Working on improving your weaknesses will not get you the same return for your time and energy compared to working on improving your strengths.**

All of us do not want to waste our time, money and energy. Continuing to improve your weaknesses is wasting your time, money and energy. Stop! How much have you already spent on 'areas to improve' over your life, and what has that done for your self-esteem – your paycheck – your advancement – your retirement? Probably not that much! To see a real difference in your life, concentrate on your strengths!

Assume that one of your talents is that you are naturally competitive. You compare yourself to others regularly. When you compete and win, it feels great. Take time to improve your talent by studying why you won rather than why you lost. Mentor someone to improve his/her skills and talents. Teaching usually results in you becoming better – because you must teach it to someone else. Constantly visualize yourself as a winner in your goals and objectives. This positive self-image will further strengthen your positive mental attitude.

How do you view failure? If you think, *"I am a failure"* then, you have just re-enforced negativity into your subconscious mind. If you view failure as *"I failed that test or competition"* then, it is a statement of failure, and it is not taken personally or with emotion into your subconscious mind. Again, analyze why you failed the test or competition. If you had it to do over again, what would you change? Do you have the right skill sets to win the next time you compete? If not, what are you going to do about it? Don't tell yourself, *"I can't afford it!"* Tell yourself, *"How can I afford it!"* and let your subconscious mind work overtime to find ways for you to attain that which you need.

No Matter What You Can Do It

Your comfort zone rules your life. Your comfort zone is defined as the total of all your activities, your time, your energy, your family, your friends, your work, your day-to-day routine, etc. You have priorities for work, family, friends, leisure activities, TV, etc. You most likely have friends with similar interests because 'likes' attract each other. It is said that the average of your ten closest friends' salaries is close to your own salary. Salary is only one measurement in your comfort zone. Many people remain comfortable and find out later in life that they had not planned well enough.

Some people may say, *"So what if I'm comfortable!"* It just means that they are defined by those boundaries and will not take the time to do the things they really need to do to make significant positive changes in their lives. As Dave Ramsey says, *"Live like no one else now so that you can live like no one else later."* Do you have an extra hour a day to spend working on your own self-improvement? If not, do you defer it to another time when you can make the time; or, do you ask yourself, *"How can I find the time to do this?"* When you start asking that kind of question you are starting to push the boundaries of your comfort zone. Your subconscious mind will figure out how to find the time or how to afford it.

You must pay the price to change for the better. Just like someone overweight or out of shape – it did not happen overnight, and you cannot fix it overnight. You must recognize it for what it is.

I have found the easiest thing for me to gain time daily is to give up TV. I grew up with TV. I cannot remember not having a TV, and not watching it as I grew up. I became addicted to TV. Even today, if it is on, I will watch it. I must make sure it is off and stays off. Does that mean I never watch TV? No. I just choose that special show or event to watch and insist on the discipline to watch that and only that. It is so easy to spend hours watching TV. I know people addicted to their computers, to shopping, to talking on the phone, etc. They spend inordinate amounts of time on-line, at the mall, talking to their friends. Ask yourself the basic question, *"What value did I get out of what I just spent the past hour or more doing?"* **If it does not add value to you, your family or your future, why are you investing that much time?**

Eliminating or greatly reducing TV also removes a significant amount of negativity from your subconscious mind. Less than one percent of our lives is bombarded with positivity. Eliminating a little negativity starts to balance the equation more in your favor. Can you live without seeing a fire on TV, or a police chase, or some animals that have been mistreated? Can you be just as aware of those things by catching the headlines and not reading the whole article or watching the entire expose on television? Won't some of your friends tell you about something if you missed it? When I surf the net for news I look at the clock on the computer and mentally challenge myself to 'x' number of minutes for each site that I go to. If I allow three minutes per site, then I must look at the headlines and figure out what is important for me to read thoroughly. Most of the time, I will find something that really looks good, and I do not want to make the time now to read it. I hit the print button and save that article for a time when I can read it later.

Become self-aware of who you are so that you can begin to make the changes necessary in your life to become a better you. Look at your comfort zone and make the hard decisions as to what is more important. You do not have to make a major change overnight, but you do need to make a **NO MATTER WHAT** decision to start – at least incrementally on the transition in your life that counts. Look at where you spend your time and energy.

Ask yourself what value are you getting in return for your time several times a day? Look at improving your strengths and viewing failure objectively. Those two things alone will make a major change in your life and improve your lifestyle down the road. Recognize negativity in everything you see, hear and read and assess it for what it is, rather than letting it emotionally affect your subconscious mind. Reduce the negativity in your life that continually bombards you from things over which you have control.

Smokey the Bear said, *"Only YOU Can Prevent Forest Fires!"* A corollary is, 'Only YOU Can Prevent Your Own Failure!' Remember you are the only person who is in charge of your life! You are the only person who can change your life.

In 480 BC, a battle took place in Greece between the Spartans and the Persians. Xerxes was the leader of the Persians. King Leonidas was the leader of the Spartans. Many of us have seen one or two movies regarding the Battle at Thermopylae. Some of us may have read books about it. History is vague on some points of the battle, but the plan was for a force of 300 Spartans plus some supporting warfighters to hold the Persian army for the rest of Greece to evacuate. The Persians had been reported to have a force of 200,000 to 400,000 in their army and a similar number in their navy. The Spartans numbered 300 and were reinforced with another 6000 to 7000 troops. The timing for this battle was not good for the Greeks. They were celebrating the festival of Carneia, and all military activity was forbidden during this time. Additionally, the Olympic Games were also scheduled to commence shortly, and military activity was also forbidden during the Olympic Games.

A small Spartan force was selected to block the pass at Thermopylae. They were to hold the pass until the Spartan army could join them. King Leonidas visited the Oracle at Delphi before leaving for Thermopylae. The Oracle's prophecy was:

O ye men who dwell in the streets of broad Lacedaemon!

Either your glorious town shall be sacked by the children of Perseus,

Or, in exchange, must all through the whole Laconian country

Mourn the loss of a king, descendant of great Heracles.

Because of the prophecy, King Leonidas selected only Spartans with living sons to fight with him at Thermopylae. The pass at Thermopylae is extremely narrow and could be held by a much smaller military force. The geography favored the Greeks in a 'holding' situation. King Leonidas positioned troops to ensure that the Persians would funnel through the passes at Thermopylae and Artemisium. The pass was so narrow that only one chariot could pass through it at a time. On one side were cliffs and the other side the Gulf of Malia.

The Spartans held out for three days. If they could have held out for a longer period, it is conceivable that Xerxes would have had to turn around because he would not have had the water and food to maintain his army. The Spartans held their ground well and attrition each day cut down their number. King Leonidas ordered all the support troops to take the wounded and depart before the final battle.

No Matter What You Can Do It

The Battle at Thermopylae is probably the most famous battle in ancient European history. The advantage of training, equipment and use of terrain became force multipliers for the Spartans. The importance of selecting this story as an example of **NO MATTER WHAT** goes a little deeper for me. What happens when fear prevents me from making a **NO MATTER WHAT** decision? *Fall back to Comfort zone*

Obviously, the Spartans knew when they volunteered that there were tremendous odds in dying. Fear of dying is a fear that few of us can face well. How did the Spartans overcome their fear of dying? Steven Pressfield in his book, *Gates of Fire*, discusses 'fear' in many respects. He discusses fear conquering fear – sort of a fear of failure. Could not someone compare fear of failure to courage and say that courage overcomes fear. One could, but courage might outweigh fear for a few, but not for the many – even with veterans fighting at their side. If it is not fear of failure or courage in the face of fear, what else is there?

Passion is sometimes given as an antidote for fear – if you are so passionate about something, you can use your passion to overcome your fear. Does that make sense when the result is death? Maybe, but only for a few. There are those who revel in battle and are passionate about the odds and the kill. They are blinded to fear of death by their passion for winning in battle. Some of us call that 'valor' today. It is hard to raise your level of courage to your level of passion and maintain it through the heights of many battles knowing that the overwhelming odds are against you.

The Spartans trained their troops from a very young age. They were taught how to fight and what was expected of them. Training was ingrained in their psyches. They trained the way they fought. During the year, they would train 24 hours a day over hilly and mountainous terrain. They worked as a whole – if one person fell or slipped behind, another automatically slipped in where needed. If there were brush or large boulders and they could not be walked over, it was assumed that they were the bodies of their dead enemy, and the formation moved around them and reformed. They moved as one and fought and thought as one. They trained so hard they did not have time to think about their fear of dying. Their training became so natural that they developed a love for battle and to prove them worthy.

So, does love conquer fear? I believe it does. Ask people today who used to be afraid of something – say public speaking. Do they fear it today as they used to? No, they relish getting in front of an audience – they 'love' what they used to 'fear'. They overcame their fear through training and more training. If you are afraid to pick up the phone and call someone, or to perform some function that must be done for you to succeed, then you can overcome it one step at a time. Nothing will compete more efficiently and effectively in combating your fear than to confront it through training. You have access to mentors, family, friends, books, CDs, DVDs, seminars, personal coaching, etc. to assist you in your journey.

Break them down into small tasks, and begin to crunch away one bite at a time. Analyze your fear. Is it a fear or failure? Is it a fear of embarrassment? **Your self-belief, how your subconscious mind views you, will avoid risk rather than reap rewards. Your subconscious mind does not want you to do something that is dangerous, embarrassing or humiliating to you.**

You can change your subconscious mind through structured practice and training. You can set up a positive program to gradually whittle down the negativity and fear so that you can overcome your fear in the long run. Conquering your fear of failure is critical to you achieving your **NO MATTER WHAT** goal.

Summary:

Your 6th **NO MATTER WHAT** decision – Determine what's important in my life and how can I get started?

- Your subconscious mind only understands commands in the present tense. It does not understand future tense.

- Your subconscious mind can re-enforce positivity and negativity with equal ease.

- **Guideline #64:** Assess the constraints in your life – what is holding you back – be honest!

- **Guideline #65:** Determine what negativity you can avoid – then avoid it – daily!

- **Guideline #66:** Work on your strengths – not your weaknesses.

- All of us are born with talent. We must learn skills.

- **Guideline #67:** Constantly visualize yourself as a winner.

- **Guideline #68:** View failure objectively.

- **Guideline #69:** Analyze your failures. Try a new tack. See what works. Continue until you find the solution. Learn the lesson well. Don't repeat it.

- **Guideline #70:** Don't tell yourself, "I can't afford it." Tell yourself, "How can I afford it?" Let your subconscious mind figure out how you can afford it.

- **Guideline #71:** Don't tell yourself, "I can't find the time." Tell yourself, "How can I find the time?" Allow your subconscious mind to find the solution.

- Your comfort zone rules your life.

- You must pay the price to change for the better.

- **Guideline #72:** Give up one hour of television a day. Spend the time wisely.

- **Guideline #73:** At the end of the day, ask yourself, "What value did I add to my future self today?"

- **Guideline #74:** Don't persist doing activities daily that will not add value to your life.

- **Guideline #75:** Make incremental changes daily. You don't have to make major changes or improvements overnight.

- **Guideline #76:** Determine two things that will add value to your retirement and start doing them this month.

- **Guideline #77:** Don't let negativity affect you emotionally.

- Only you can prevent your own failure.

- You are in charge of your life.

- Removing television removes a significant amount of negativity from your life.

- You control the level of negativity from your life.

- **Guideline #78:** Overcome your fears through practice and training.

- *"You make mistakes. Mistakes don't make you."* Maxwell Maltz

Self Improvement

Begin slowly and complete what you have scheduled. Assume you bought a book and had a goal of reading a book a month for a year. Halfway through the book, you get bored and decide to buy a different book. Or, maybe you talk to someone and he says that you can borrow his CD set. You stop reading and begin something else. This can be counterproductive to your long-term goals. Plan something and complete it. Change milestones only when they need to be changed.

I am not saying that you cannot <u>change your plans</u>. Be <u>committed</u> to what you are doing. Recognize a need for change when it makes sense.

<u>Time</u> is going to be more critical for your mindset change than budget. There are many free articles, reports, blogs, e-zines on the Internet. Libraries have books and CD programs. Many in the

Brotherhood of Prosperity have free daily or weekly e-mail tips and newsletters on self-improvement and related topics.

An easy assignment daily would be to spend fifteen minutes researching a topic of interest. I find it difficult to read for a long time on a monitor. Short articles are easy, but sometimes the length or complexity leads me to print it out for future reading. Most people find their daily disposable time is constantly filled up with distractions. **Select your distractions wisely!**

Allow me to describe a typical 'distraction' that I encounter often at home. I am in my bedroom and going to the kitchen to get a glass of water. As I leave my bedroom, I see something sitting on a shelf, and decide that it should not be there. I grab it and take it back into the bedroom. Leaving my bedroom again, I find another opportunity to steal time from my schedule, and I select that distraction also. My original mission was to get a glass of water, but it might have been aborted, or certainly delayed because I chose to act on other non-planned events. It happens to all of us.

I used to get frustrated because I had specific daily goals to accomplish and would jump at targets of opportunity that would only take a few seconds to handle. That one distraction would lead to another and, suddenly, I had multiple distractions vying for my time. The original goal was still there, but it was not being done and my schedule for the day was slipping.

I found the easiest way to handle this dilemma was to take heed of an old saying – *If you can't beat them, join them!* Now my daily schedule has a couple slots set aside for distractions. They are inserted at appropriate times to facilitate other activities. The distractions are now selected wisely and I have found that when my time is up, I have worked on what I needed to do and can move on quickly to the next thing on my daily mission list. I no longer feel frustrated with unplanned breaks in my daily mission. **Choose your distractions wisely because you cannot re-coop the time you lost.**

By now you should be planting seeds of positive change into your subconscious mind.

- **Read, listen to CDs or view DVDs, and talk to successful people and solicit their advice.**
- **Control your culture of comfort – your personal comfort zone.**
- **Think more positively to wipe out your existing negative programming**
- **Think more critically and restructure your thoughts to – how can I afford it? Or, how can I make time for it?**
- **Develop your financial acuity.**
- **View failure objectively.**

No Matter What You Can Do It

These are just a few of the things you have learned so far. You are beginning the process of transitioning from understanding how you change your subconscious processes and becoming more self-aware of who you are and where you want to go. The next transition is to establish an action plan for you to complete your mindset transition.

Your past does not determine your future. This is extremely important since past failures and perceptions of what you have done – or failed to do – are unimportant. You can reprogram your subconscious mind to filter those events out of consideration and literally begin anew.

Anthony Robbins said, *"If you talk about it, it's a dream. If you envision it, it's possible. But, if you schedule it, it's real."* Start with your dream. Back when we were kids we used to dream all the time – maybe you wanted to be an astronaut, or a ballerina, or a cowboy, or a professional basketball player. You all had dreams. As you grew, sometimes those dreams were trampled on by your family, friends and society to a point that they no longer seemed worthy of your consideration. Some of you had parents who told you that whatever you wanted to do in life was attainable – if you applied yourselves and worked hard for it. Take a moment and go back to your dream years. Rekindle in that part of your brain what you really wanted in life. Is it much different from what you want today? Today most of you still have dreams of what you want to accomplish in your lives and do not know how to do it.

Determine the 'root cause' of your dream to find the real reason why. What is your 'bottom line' WHY? Does it give you that 'buzz' when you think about it? Is it just a 'black and white' picture, or is it a picture bursting with color?

Dreams tend to grow with time. Some people will progress from financial freedom to early retirement, to travel, to helping others, etc. As your dreams get <u>big enough</u>, then a new characteristic happens in your subconscious mind – your dream becomes an objective that your subconscious mind must determine a <u>way to achieve it</u>. The bigger and the harder it is, the harder your brain will work to find the solution. Use your subconscious mind to work <u>24 hours a day</u> to come up with your dream solution.

Alice in Wonderland had a problem in selecting the right road – she did not have a destination – so any road would get her there. Now is the time to determine which road you need to choose. You have given some thought to a dream or dreams you would like to accomplish. Write them down – not type them, but <u>handwrite</u> them. Again, the power is in transferring those thoughts from your brain through your hand onto paper and seeing them as they are transcribed. Take one of your dreams – one that you know is reasonably <u>easy</u> to achieve. For example, it might be something like having a million dollars, or ten million dollars in your retirement portfolio. This is not a big deal unless you are 87 years old, not working and living on Social Security.

When do you need those million dollars? It is probably in 'x' number of years. You have a target and a deadline.

What do you need to do today, tomorrow, this week, this month, this year to make that goal? Write it down below your target with dates. Allow your subconscious mind to begin working on your solution. Do not skimp on details. It is easy to determine that a million dollars divided by 'x' is what you need each year.

What do you need to do today to begin that process? Yoda, from Star Wars, said, *'Do or do not, there is no try!'* You are not going to try to do something – you are going to do it. You are in control and you are responsible.

What programs and options do you have to meet your million-dollar goal? You can add a few dollars out of each paycheck but that probably will not meet your annual requirement to have a million dollars in 'x' years. You need to look at your current expenditures and restructure those. Look at investment options or other sources of income. It is not difficult, just different from your normal thought process. It is not something you talk about with your friends and family. You must begin today thinking about what you can do with what you have - and - what you want to achieve on your road to success. The written details of each objective provide more clarity for your subconscious mind to assist you. The more emotion associated with your target also provides your subconscious mind with the 'need' to make it happen.

Set hard measurements for each of your goals. If your goal at the end of one month was to know three investment options, to have a written budget, and to prioritize your disposable income - then it is easy to say you have done that or you have not. Keep score along the way. If you need to restructure your schedule – then do so. It is only a plan and <u>you control your plan</u>. Maybe your target, plan or deadline was too aggressive to start. Reassess it once you have accumulated some knowledge. <u>Adjust</u> your plan accordingly.

Many of us, I included, get ingrained in **analysis-paralysis**. We would prefer to study something rather than do it – to execute our plan. That is why you need the deadlines to ensure that you hold yourself accountable. When you write your goals do not use the words: <u>**Try or trying, should, or would like to**</u>. **Remove those limiting words (try, should, would like) from your vocabulary**. Do it! Don't try, as Yoda or Nike would say. **Act and observe your results. This is key.**

No Matter What You Can Do It

I mentioned earlier learning from your successes / actions / mistakes / failures. They are great opportunities to be better than the average bear.

Most **NO MATTER WHAT** examples that I have researched involved individuals. Some involved teams or organizations. I think the most impressive **NO MATTER WHAT** decision was made by President Kennedy when he delivered a speech to a joint session of Congress on May 25, 1961. He said, *"I believe that this nation should commit itself to achieving the goal, before this decade is out, of landing a man on the Moon and returning him safely to Earth."* He asked for $1,700,000,000.00 (one point seven billion dollars) to fund the program initially and wanted another $9,000,000,000.00 (nine billion dollars) for the next five years.

Russia's Yuri Gagarin became the first man in space the month before President Kennedy's speech. The Russians were 'miles' ahead of the United States in their space program. It was a 'catch-up' job from the beginning. I have read several books covering various aspects of America's space program, and the one I like the best is *Failure Is Not an Option* by Gene Kranz, former Flight Director for NASA. The title explicitly tells us that **NO MATTER WHAT**, we will put a man on the moon by the end of the 1960's.

The entire effort that resulted in Neil Armstrong stepping on the moon on July 21, 1969, committed our congress, our military, our technology infrastructure, and many other supporting organizations. In 1961, the United States had missiles – but not missiles that could put a man safely into space. Many great minds worked together to develop the program that would gradually launch missiles successfully, then put a man into space, then have man orbit the earth, then have man orbit the moon, and finally have man land on the moon. Even today, I am amazed at the effort that had to happen in a time crunch to be as successful as it was.

Failure is not an option when you want to put a man on the moon safely and return him to our home planet. Individual failure has been discussed in this home study course – something that permeates our being, our mind, and our psyche. Failure now involved our nation. How did the American Space program prevent failure – **NO MATTER WHAT**?

The goals were set.

- Launch man into space
- Land a man on the moon
- Return him to earth safely

The mission requirements to do that involved a myriad of complex tasks – selection of missiles, astronauts, training, communications, backups and backups to backups. Each step along the way listed critical requirements that must be done to go the next step. This is like what you do as you work your way to your goals and dreams.

One of my skills is in the field of reliability engineering. Reliability is the ability of a system to perform its functions as designed – under stated conditions for a specified time. The stated conditions can be in a normal or hostile environment. NASA conducted failure modes and effects analyses. Failure modes and effects analyses are analytical procedures used to look for any potential failure mechanism. You classify that failure mechanism for the impact to success – minor or major degradation, catastrophic failure, loss of human life. You look at failure causes and impacts – what can cause this circuit or equipment to fail, what can be done to eliminate it, or what 'work-around' can be put in place to mitigate a failure. You want to know in advance the effect of each potential failure before it occurs, and what you can do to prevent it or to minimize it. You must know what impact any level of failure has on the mission, and what options you have for each occurrence. Options may be different if the failure occurred before launch, during launch, in earth orbit, in lunar orbit, on the moon, or on re-entry.

You do not go to that extreme when you plan for your goals – but you do not have loss of human life resulting from your failure. The two significant issues that I gleaned from my studies of America's space program were planning and training.

Through planning, you want to know in advance what your objectives are – set them in concrete and keep them constantly in mind. Update them as more reliable data becomes available. The same rule applies to us as individuals.

Training is something that you should add to your schedule. You must be in a continual learning mode – to develop your personal growth plan that keeps you current with your quest for bigger and better.

In NASA's case, the training was extreme. Every system (electrical, hydraulic, pneumatic, software, life support, etc.) was analyzed thoroughly and programs were established to determine what could fail and what would happen. Then monitoring systems had to be installed to tell ground and flight personnel what was going on before and during the flight. It was critical that everyone know if a circuit shut down early or if equipment did not respond when directed or expected.

Training programs were developed that took the ground and flight personnel through a perfect launch. Then a repeat was commenced in which a minor 'glitch' was discovered at some point in time. How would the ground and flight personnel respond? If it was correct – great! If it was not, what were the results? Did the test have to be repeated? In many cases, the test was repeated and other 'glitches' were included to add confusion and time pressures. Before any launch could be 'signed off' as ready to launch, the ground and flight crews had to pass every test along the way. They had to know how to recognize and how to respond to any problem. This was not just the personnel at Cape Canaveral and Houston and in the spacecraft, but everywhere around the world who monitored the progress of the space flight. It would not do to have only Houston personnel qualified to recognize a problem when it occurred 10,000 miles away. Australia ground monitoring personnel would have to react to a sensor warning that something was not perfect. Their training had to be as complete as Houston's personnel.

In addition to being able to recognize a problem when it occurred, there had to be the 'right' response to the problem. In some cases, a system or component could be shut down. In other cases, teams from various civilian companies and universities were asked to investigate, evaluate and recommend a solution. When a live mission was underway, the deadline to respond was within hours, especially if a problem occurred that had not been analyzed in advance.

The mission control specialists initially operated without the benefit of computers – they did not exist when the space program got started. Many calculations were done by hand. When a trajectory had to be 'recalculated,' it had to be done in such a way as to provide enough time for that updated information to be transmitted to the spacecraft. The astronauts had to verify that it was received correctly, and had to be ready to implement the new time event. Communications early in the space program were rudimentary – at best. There were no satellites or cables providing instantaneous contact with stations in Africa, Australia or to ships at sea. The whole concept of keeping everyone apprised of what was happening at any instant in the flight is mind shattering. While all this was going on, the Russians were still one or two steps ahead of the United States in their conquest of space. Just when NASA thought they would equal a record set by the Russians, the Russians would make another leap ahead in their space program.

Most everyone knows of the explosion on the Apollo 13 mission. This mission is a **NO MATTER WHAT** example. Reports, articles, books and documentaries/movies have portrayed this event probably more than any other space flight other than the actual landing on the moon. The type of catastrophe that happened with Apollo 13 was never contemplated – certainly not with the overall impact of damage to the spacecraft. Just about every manned space launch had some **NO MATTER WHAT** decisions that had to be made to correct something to bring our astronauts home safely. Fortunately, the right people were skilled, knowledgeable and ready to make those decisions.

No Matter What You Can Do It

Summary:

- **Guideline #79:** Complete what you schedule. Don't make changes arbitrarily.

- **Guideline #80:** Be committed to what you decide.

- Time is more critical than budget to change your mindset.

- **Guideline #81:** Select your distractions wisely.

- Distractions lead to major waste of time.

- Your past does not determine your present.

- Remember your early dreams – determine, if you can, why you changed them.

- **Guideline #82:** Determine the root cause - the underlying 'why' of why you want to achieve your dreams/goals. It must evoke emotion within you.

- **Guideline #83:** Ensure you have targets and deadlines for your milestones and goals.

- **Guideline #84:** Determine what you need to start your journey today and tomorrow. Don't wait too far into the future to begin.

- The more details describing what you want to achieve in life – the higher the probability of success.

- **Guideline #85:** Prioritize your disposable income.

- **Guideline #86:** Reassess plans after you have accumulated enough information to make changes.

- **Guideline #87:** Avoid analysis-paralysis.
- **Guideline #88:** Don't use the words: Try, Should, Would Like, etc. Check your vocabulary to ensure you use the words you want to use.
- **Guideline #89:** Remain in a continual learning mode.
- **Guideline #90:** Keep current in your quest for the gold. Know enough to progress all the way to your goal and past.

"Never give in, never, never, never, never." Winston Churchill

"Dreams don't work unless you do." Peter Daniels

"Don't tell yourself how big your problems are – tell your problems how big you are." Bill Bartmann

One of these days – is none of these days. English Proverb

"Opportunity is missed by most people because it is dressed in overalls and looks like work." Thomas Alva Edison

"I will prepare and someday my chance will come." Abraham Lincoln

"We are all faced with a series of great opportunities brilliantly disguised as impossible situations." Charles R. Swindoll

No Matter What You Can Do It

Planning

We are creatures of habit – that is how we got into our current comfort zones. Now you know how to change. Treat your action plan with commitment and belief. You should have an action plan for the year, for the next month, for the next week, for tomorrow and for today.

At the end of the day, reflect on your successes in accomplishing your daily goals and on what did and did not go right. Understand what caused you to make and/or miss that deadline. You are reviewing your day critically for improvement, for maintaining a positive self-image, and for making progress on your short and long-term goals.

At the end of the day, adjust tomorrow's schedule to reflect what <u>absolutely needs to be done</u> and write next to it – <u>NO MATTER WHAT!</u> If you do not learn anything else well in this book, this action must be taken. Assess your day and plan tomorrow. Make it a habit to know where you are on your road to success. If you do not, then distractions and frustration will lead you astray! Know what your number one priority is for tomorrow and let your subconscious mind attack it for you and make you better prepared to complete it.

In the evening before going to bed, read aloud your action list for tomorrow. It will give your subconscious mind something to think about while you are sleeping. In the morning grab your list and repeat, again out loud, the goals for today. Ensure that you have them prioritized! Reading aloud is critical.

Ask yourself if there is any specific knowledge that you need to complete your goals. If so, how do you get it? Look at your day and anticipate constraints and challenges. If you know, in advance, how to deal with a constraint – when it appears it is easier to deal with it. Constraints could be unplanned visitors, phone calls, e-mails, etc. Some people set aside two to four times a day for emails or returning phone calls.

Incremental growth is easier to sustain and leads to the successful achievement of long-term goals. A Chinese Proverb says, *'Be not afraid of going slowly; be afraid only of standing still.'* A little done each day will work wonders. Jeff Olson wrote the book, *'The Slight Edge.'* It is an excellent book. He uses an example of a penny a day doubled. If someone offered you a penny a day to go to work and he would double it each day for a month – would you do it? The first day you would earn a penny. The next day you would earn two cents. The following day you would earn four cents. It does not sound like it is worth it – does it? On the last day of the month, you would have earned more than a million dollars.

It is the incremental efforts put forth daily that pays dividends in the future. Likewise, a slight negative variation done daily yields negative results magnified. That is probably how most of us got into our current comfort zones.

Incremental growth works great, but you need to have measurements to know if you are deviating from your goal. Review your previous deadlines and see if there is a pattern of **why** something was missed. If you understand why you could not make that deadline, then you are mastering control over your future.

You are in a constant battle against the negative influences in your life. But, with practice and discipline, you have the tools to fight through those negative influences and make progress towards your dreams.

You need to be a continual student of learning

> **from your past,**
> **from your failures and**
> **from your successes**

No Matter What You Can Do It

Your motto should be '**Never Stop Learning!**' Many of you find out that as you approach the 70-80% of your goal you may become less excited about achieving it. Assume your goal was to read a book a month for the next year. After six months, you are slightly ahead of schedule and the excitement of achieving that goal starts to lessen. It is natural. It is also the best time to assess whether that goal is as optimal today as it was when you set it. It is an excellent time to revise the goal – either in terms of <u>what</u> needs to be accomplished or in terms of <u>when</u> it will be completed.

You will fail often as you progress toward your goals. That is why it is important to continually measure your progress so that you know where you are along the way.

Winston Churchill said, *"Success is the ability to move from one failure to the next with enthusiasm."* Recognize your failure objectively. You are the CEO, Vice President, Director, Owner, Manager, Engineer, Technician, and Worker Bee of your life. Sometimes you dream and other times you are doing, managing, measuring, planning, etc. Regardless of what hat you are wearing, you must act on a **consistent** basis. The action must be the **correct action**.

Look at an analogy of a golfer. The golfer goes to a practice range and hits a couple of buckets of balls. Does that make the golfer a better golfer? Not necessarily. If the golfer did not observe what he was doing wrong and make the proper corrections, then all the golfer did was to act. Do not confuse doing something as doing something correctly.

There is an adage – Practice Makes Perfect. It should be Perfect Practice Makes Perfect. You must learn along the way what is working and what is not working. Sometimes you must clamp down on the task at hand and say, **NO MATTER WHAT,** I will get this done!

General George Patton said that success is measured by how far you bounce back after hitting bottom. Frustration will accompany failure and add to the negativity in your life. So long as the failure is judged objectively – *I failed that task or that deadline* – it is just that – a statement of fact. **Never accept the thought that you are a failure at what you are doing.**

You might be too ambitious or you might select too many distractions. However, just a short while ago, you did not know the **secret of changing your mindset by continually reprogramming your subconscious mind**. The acts of measuring, assessing, adjusting, making decisions, and taking responsibility - just as hitting a golf ball - gets more comfortable after hundreds and hundreds of swings.

It still amazes me how we tend to sneak back to our comfort zones when things appear to be out of control. They would not appear to be out of control if you were not trying to change. Knowing what you know now, would you still be satisfied with the status quo and living another day in the Poverty Industrial Complex? H. Ross Perot said – *"Most people give up just when they are about to achieve success. They quit on the one-yard line. They give up at the last minute of the game, one foot from a winning touchdown."*

It is like climbing a hill in the fog. You cannot see the top of the hill – you are always going upward. The climb is hard and boring and there is not much to show for positive achievement. You tire quickly and the scenery – the fog – never changes, so you start having self-doubt. That self-doubt starts erasing some of the self-esteem you have built up and you begin rationalizing that maybe this was not for you. When you get a chance, Google 'facing the giants-football'. There is a short film clip based on the movie with the same title. It is a great cure for self-doubt.

The natural solution to this milestone in your journey may be to reassess everything. Maybe the goal – the big dream – the thing you have always wanted, was not big enough for you to take it seriously; or, maybe it really was not realistic, or maybe you did not attach enough emotion to it to stimulate your subconscious mind. <u>Do not confuse talent with skill</u>. You can dream about being a Michael Jordan or a Wayne Gretzky, but you need the talent to build on to get there. Maybe it is time to reassess your goal and your yardstick. You may not have mastered programming your subconscious mind yet. Maybe a solution is to supercharge your subconscious mind with a **NO MATTER WHAT** decision to break through.

Quitting is easy. **Failure can be accepted, but quitting is a personal decision.** Note: There are isolated situations where quitting might be the right decision. Only you will know for sure. Breaking through your frustration is more difficult when you take it personally instead of objectively. You have the tools and the knowledge now to accomplish what you want to do.

Most people probably do not remember the **four-inch space flight** from Cape Canaveral on November 21, 1960. A Mercury-Redstone 1 missile malfunctioned at lift-off and lifted four inches off the ground, then the main engines shut down, and the missile landed back on the ground in its original launch configuration. The missile was still armed and full of fuel sitting on the ramp. The umbilical cable had disconnected from the missile. The Mercury capsule sensed the booster's engine shutdown and acted accordingly – it had sent a command to jettison the escape tower. The escape tower was launched – as programmed – and there was fear for a couple minutes that it might come back to earth and land on top of the Mercury-Redstone missile. It missed the launch complex by 1200 feet. The capsule sensed no further acceleration and acted as if it were in the recovery phase of the mission and deployed its parachute.

No Matter What You Can Do It

The missile was sitting on the ramp – full of fuel with a large parachute 'dangling' from the top of the capsule. There was fear that the wind could catch the parachute and topple the missile. The booster's destruct system was armed and there was no way to shut it down. No one knew what to do! They thought they had been trained as well as they could have been and were dumbfounded to find out that they were nowhere near ready for space flight. This was one of the first missions launched by NASA. Many lessons were learned. The important thing for the United States was that lessons were learned. We, as NASA, must also learn lessons as things go wrong in our journey.

Jump ahead a few years to 1969 – the year that NASA landed a man on the moon. Simulation training had been perfected, skills were honed and knowledge was now converted into wisdom by many of those who survived the rigors of space launches. The training for a moon mission had extra, added complexity in that there was a three-second delay in communications going each way because of the distance involved (The moon averages 238,712 miles away from the earth and the speed of communications is approximately 186,282.3960 miles/second.) You must allow the 'transit time' for communications to get from earth to the spacecraft and confirmation back to earth. Early testing had shown that this was a major problem. Eventually, it was overcome and people were planning for the delay and were getting their heads ahead of the time delay to respond properly. The training was intensive because Apollo 11 was going to orbit the moon and eventually land a man on the moon.

On the last day of training, the simulation team went to an extreme level to test the mission controllers in their ability to handle unique and challenging problems. During a simulated lunar module orbit of the moon, the simulation team sent a 'signal' to mission control that indicated a computer restart on the lunar module. The alarm code that the mission controllers received had never been tested previously. They identified the code as 'executive overflow – no vacant areas.' This meant that the computer was overloaded. The lunar module would no longer be able to complete the jobs during a major computer cycle. NASA had instituted 'rules' for specific situations during a launch, flight and recovery. There were no rules for this type of problem. No one knew exactly what to do. Everything else seemed to be working properly and the alarm they received could be valid or invalid – who knew? The initial analysis was that the computer was working harder than it should have been and for an unknown reason. The computer indicated that something was not being done because it was 'overloaded,' yet all indications were that everything else was fine. The computer kept going through restarts and sending alarms as mission control began to panic. Thus, an ABORT command was given. Fortunately, this was in a simulation. The real mission had not been launched yet. Aborts were rarely given and this was unusual. When the lunar module is orbiting the moon, you don't want to abort the mission without a lot of prior planning and forethought. Aborts had to be planned and executed with perfect timing.

The after-action debriefing from the simulation team was that an abort should not have been called and they discussed their reasoning. The mission control staff had 'guessed' what to do, and had also violated one of their own critical rules of having, at least, two separate and distinct sensors/cues verifying a problem before initiating an abort command. The end-result was that this alarm code could be ignored if other indications were normal. The mission control team thought that they were not as prepared as they should have been and requested additional training the next day to work further on this type of problem. If you have men in orbit around the moon you do not want to guess what action to take – you must know immediately any alarm that might surface and be prepared to address it properly.

On July 20, 1969, Apollo 11 launched from Cape Canaveral and was uneventful. The mission progressed and the lunar module was orbiting the moon awaiting final GO for landing. Before the GO was given, a radar-tracking problem was found – the radar could not verify height and distance. This problem was addressed and just before a GO was given the exact same alarm code that was 'tested' on the last day of simulation popped up. Buzz Aldrin reported this alarm to mission control - it was the same alarm code the mission controllers had in training after they had failed the simulation. Based on the training the mission control specialists had received and their knowledge of the systems, they could 'discount' this alarm and keep vigilant for any other supporting information that would or could validate this alarm. The final GO was given for moon landing and the rest is history. Had they not known and practiced with this particular alarm code, it is not certain today if Apollo 11 would have landed first on the moon. Less than four months later, another American crew landed on the moon.

The mission control staff in Houston, Texas made the right **NO MATTER WHAT** decisions to successfully land a man on the moon within a decade of President Kennedy's speech to Congress.

Summary:

Your 7th **NO MATTER WHAT** decision: Write **NO MATTER WHAT** on your number one short-term priority. Tell yourself that you must do this **NO MATTER WHAT**!

- **Guideline # 91:** Have an Action Plan for the week, the month and the year.

- **Guideline #92:** Treat you Action Plan with commitment and belief.

- **Guideline #93:** Understand why you missed a deadline.

- **Guideline #94:** Know your #1 priority for tomorrow before you go to bed.

- **Guideline #95:** Read your Action Plan for tomorrow and next week before going to bed.

- **Guideline #96:** Read your Action Plan for the day when you wake up in the morning.

- **Guideline #97:** Assess what specific knowledge you will need to complete your milestones and goals. Ensure you complete the training or study in time to complete your milestone or goal.

- Incremental growth is easy to sustain for success or failure. Incremental positive growth leads to success. Incremental negative growth keeps you in your comfort zone.

- **Guideline #98:** Measure yourself on your journey to success. Make sure you are using the right yardstick and timepiece.

- **Guideline #99:** Never stop learning.

- **Guideline #100:** Reassess your long-term goals every six months. Adjust only if necessary based on accurate information obtained during that time.

- **Guideline #101:** Ensure you are taking the <u>correct action</u>. Otherwise, you will be taking <u>corrective action</u>. Corrective action is the action taken to correct what was done in error the first time. If correct action is taken initially, then there will be no need to take any further action.

- Perfect Practice makes Perfect

- You are out of control only because you are trying to change. If you were in control, you would be enjoying your comfort zone.

- Self-doubt erases self-esteem. When self-doubt enters the door – reassess your goal – is it realistic – is it crystal clear – do you have enough emotion attached to it?

- **Guideline #102:** Don't confuse talent with skill.

- **Guideline #103:** Failure can be accepted.

- Quitting is a personal choice.

"Opportunity meets you at your level of expectation." Bill Bartmann

"If you believe, then all things are possible." Mark 9:23

No Matter What You Can Do It

"The greatest barrier to success is the fear of failure." Sven Goren Eriksson

"Fear of failure must never be a reason not to try something." Frederick Smith

Measuring

Many people think that they can live on a couple of million dollars in their 401K plan, plus some Social Security income. Inflation, market fluctuations and unplanned expenses affect your total investment. If you are planning to live on 'x' dollars when you are 60 years of age, will it be sufficient to continue living on at 85 years of age, or even at 95 years of age?

The questions for retirement income really are

- **What lifestyle can you afford?**
- **Are you happy with that lifestyle?**
- **Will that lifestyle grow or decline over time?**

Your future finances and quality of life depend on the choices and decisions you make today. One of the things our educational system <u>does not do</u> is to educate people on basic finance. Einstein is credited with saying that the greatest force in the universe is compound interest. It is unlikely he said it, but it gives credence to the power of compound interest. Anyone who has made house payments for years can understand this concept intimately – you pay, and pay, and pay, and pay, and still have a large debt.

What are your real expectations for your retirement? Have you thought that far ahead yet? The earlier you know what you want, the earlier you can begin your journey. Most people will spend more time looking for a new home or a new job than they will planning for their financial future. Is there something magical about numbers that keeps many of us from approaching that endeavor? Part of it is the **poverty mindset** that I brought up earlier.

You have been conditioned all your lives to believe that money is the root of all evil or some other trite saying. That saying goes, 'It is the love of money that is the root of all evil.' However, you have been brainwashed through your formative years to not pursue that topic. You choose not to study it in your spare time. Most of you do not even seek conversations about it.

To survive through your retirement, you need to improve your financial acuity. You need to understand the basics so that you can compare and contrast various options that you will have extra money that can be invested. You want to be able to converse intelligently with financial planners – or, at least, discuss your financial needs in much the same way you would talk to your doctor or lawyer for medical and legal issues. You should strive to be at an <u>intermediate level of understanding</u> of financial competence to ask the right questions and understand the answers. You should also know with clarity what you personally need to do for your retirement. Put it near the top of the list for your study. Myron Golden says, *"If you don't know finance, someone else will use it against you to improve his life."*

You are in charge of your money and your life. That should be your minimum expectation. You need to know enough to make educated guesses as to which plan or option is best for you and your risk level. I mentioned earlier that an extra $200/month could make a difference in declaring bankruptcy or not. $200 a month is not a lot of money in the big scheme of things.

$200 a month is the same thing as having $50,000 in the bank drawing 4.75% interest. Is it easier to get $50,000 into your savings account, or is it easier to find another source of income that produces $200 a month?

Is it your expectation to work a second job forever? Could it be some other economic opportunity that will equate to the same thing? What is your time worth? Are there other options available to have the same income without the same time commitment?

I mentioned improving your financial acuity – learning more about money and how it multiplies and the risks associated with different types of investments. It is necessary to get a good start in this discipline. To improve many facets of your life, you must change your mindset. Studying finance is not easy, but it is doable. It is a must for you to take financial control over your life.

What can you do that is easy and you can start today to change your mindset? **Affirmations** are something you can start before you finish this book.

Affirmations are short positive statements targeted to certain beliefs that begin the reprogramming process for your subconscious mind. **They are present tense** – because your subconscious mind can only deal with the present. **They are positive** – because you want more positivity in your life. In addition, **they are personal** – they must involve you. Affirmations change your self-belief - your self-esteem over time. Affirmations change the internal image of you! This is critical to change your mindset.

Your subconscious mind automatically protects you against embarrassment and harm. It is a built-in self-protective mechanism. You can correct your subconscious mind's perception of embarrassment and harm. If your subconscious mind really believes that you will be harmed by attempting something, it will do everything it can to prevent it – thus, you will fail before you start.

No Matter What You Can Do It

You can change your subconscious mind in 21 days as Dr. Maxwell Maltz observed. Your brain learns through many processes – data from rote memorization (your early ABC's and numbers); data from your senses that you can confirm and validate as true (hot and cold, hard and soft, sharp and dull, etc.); data from your senses that you can correlate with other things you have learned in the past (something is hard or easy to do); thought progressions that have combined over time to yield new thought patterns – part of your creativity processes (mixing colors to achieve better balance in a design); and, data from other sources not detectable by our senses.

This data is stored in long-term memory and is available when needed. There are different levels of priority associated with the different data streams that are in your memory. Data is sorted as

High priority – something you need to retain for easy recall

Low priority – something that can be put into archives and retrieved less easily

Data with emotions attached to them are usually associated with high priority retrieval.

Your core self-belief comes from your emotional stockpile of data.

- *Money is the root of all evil*
- *Money doesn't grow on trees*
- *We can't afford it*

- *Math is hard*

- *I can't speak in public*

You form your psyche based on the compilation of this emotional data that has been stored in your brain over your lifetime. Most of it were stored without you making a judgment regarding its validity. Garbage-in (non-verifiable emotional input) is stored with fact. This is good for you since you can tell your subconscious mind which data to ignore/discount and which data to believe.

I mentioned earlier the necessity to define your goal or dream with as much detail and emotion as you can. Data with emotion attached to it defaults into high priority 'facts' for your subconscious mind. The repetition of data also conditions your subconscious mind to place that data for easier retrieval. The more you recall your goal or dream, and have the emotional buzz reinforcing the data, the more your subconscious mind will believe it is real and needed.

You can cancel the old emotional barriers to success you had firmly implanted in your subconscious mind by planting new seeds of success in your old garden of emotional garbage. Over time, the seeds of success will choke out the weeds of negativity and failure. Use your imagination to plant seeds of success. Think of what you want to become and it will happen. Visualize your success and you will be successful.

Affirmations are an easy way to plant seeds of success. Here are a few for your consideration:

- *I Like Me!*
- *Money Comes Easy to Me!*
- *I Aspire to Improve Every Day!*
- *I Learn from My Mistakes!*
- *I Am Committed to A Better Life for Me and My Family!*
- *I Finish What I Start!*
- *I Listen to Others!*

All of them are present tense, positive and personal. Affirmations said aloud affect your subconscious mind with more impact compared to affirmations read silently. There are additional ways of enhancing your affirmations to make the overall emotional impact on your subconscious mind greater than a single statement of affirmation. Change the personal aspect just slightly to alter the emotion and reinforce what you have planted. Such as, assume your name is John Doe or Sally Smith

- *John Doe would say - John Likes ME!*
- *Money Come Easy to John!*
- *Sally Smith would say - Sally Aspires to Improve Every Day!*

- *Sally Learns from Her Mistakes!*

Or

- *John Doe IS Committed to A Better Life for John Doe and His Family!*
- *Sally Smith Finishes What She Starts!*
- *John Doe Listens to Others!*
- *Sally Smith Learns from her Mistakes!*

Changing "I" to "John" or "John Doe" gives your subconscious mind a different recognition value. "I" is personal. John is also personal, but it comes to your subconscious mind in a somewhat different interpretation – sort of a second person affirming your affirmation. The more formal "John Doe" in the affirmation makes it strong from another outside perspective – the outside world agrees with your affirmation – so, therefore, it must be true.

Another self-improvement tool is to "handwrite" your affirmation repeatedly. The link between the hand and the pen and paper and the emotional statement being written adds credibility and emotion to your subconscious mind. Another tool would be to record your affirmations and listen to them on a regular basis. Professional athletes have been doing this for a long time.

No Matter What You Can Do It

You can use affirmations to counter the negativity that is already programmed into your subconscious mind and to build a new you in the process. Affirmations should be said aloud with feeling – believing what you are saying. They should be said multiple times during the day. They should be visible in places where you spend your time – such as your car, your nightstand, your computer, and your wallet. Handwrite them so that you have more ownership than objectively typing them. Both methods (handwriting and typing) work – one better than the other. Both can be employed in your daily affirmation ritual. Tape them to your bathroom mirror or next to your computer.

Affirmations are extremely powerful tools. Your subconscious mind can be reprogrammed in as little as 3-4 weeks if said daily with passion multiple times a day. Affirmations become the building blocks to kick-start your mindset change. Affirmations are even more powerful if said just before going to sleep. It allows your subconscious mind to focus on those last thoughts throughout the night. It forces your subconscious mind to figure our how you are going to achieve those positive statements in your life. Affirmations force-feed your subconscious mind with directions for a better life. Mohammed Ali said he was the *"Greatest"* long before he believed it.

Here is a secret to supercharge <u>one or two</u> of these affirmations. Add the words **'NO MATTER WHAT'** to the end of your affirmation. Such as:

- **I Listen to Others <u>NO MATTER WHAT!</u>**
- **I Learn from My Mistakes <u>NO MATTER WHAT!</u>**

Just those three little words cause your subconscious mind to focus like a <u>laser beam</u> on that statement and your subconscious mind brings that affirmation to the head of the list to develop a new neural path to implant into your brain. The supercharged affirmation attaches emotion to the directive and your subconscious mind goes into overdrive to respond.

Here is a little trick that I have used many, many times. Assume it is Sunday night and for whatever reason you must get up in three hours to go to work. Typically, you would look at the clock and say to yourself something like: *"I cannot believe I have to be at work in a couple of hours – I will be dragging all day – It will be a couple of days before I can catch up on my sleep and be normal again."*

You get the message – you are programming your brain for a negative response. Try the positive approach with a quick affirmation statement. Say, *"I am taking a three-hour nap."* Transitioning from a full night's sleep to a 'nap' makes your subconscious mind think that you do not need your full sleep and you will be satisfied with a nap. You continue to tell yourself: *"I wake every day refreshed and ready for another great day!"* Again, a positive statement personalized to you. Add, *"I am a professional and always work consistently with a clear focus."* Now you are telling your brain that when you work you are clear-headed – not sleepy, and that you focus on what you do.

You will be amazed how well this works. There are many variations you can use. You will wake up no worse than you would any other morning with a full sleep cycle. You go to work and discover by mid-morning that you are not nearly as tired as you thought you would be. Your subconscious mind took care of you during that three-hour nap and you reap the rewards from it. No, you cannot use this technique for thirty days in a row – your body really does get tired after a while, but you can use it multiple days in a row to get through a busy time in your life. I have used this technique many times.

In considering examples of **NO MATTER WHAT** decisions people have made when they put their lives on the line, my mind was drawn to the Checkpoint Charlie Museum I visited a few years ago in Berlin, Germany. Checkpoint Charlie was created during the Cold War and was located at the junction of Friedrichstrasse with Zimmerstrasse and Mauerstrasse. Checkpoint Charlie was one of many sector-crossing points in Berlin. The Berlin Wall separated East Berlin from West Berlin.

No Matter What You Can Do It

Checkpoint Charlie was designated as a single crossing point for foot and car traffic. Checkpoint Charlie lasted 28 years and the infrastructure changed over time to control many escape attempts.

In the Museum, there are dozens and dozens of displays and photographs of the successful and unsuccessful attempts to leave East Berlin and enter West Berlin. Escapees made their **NO MATTER WHAT** decisions understanding that if they failed they would be shot.

Two major **NO MATTER WHAT** escapes occurred before the end of World War II that were made into movies, *The Trojan Horse* and *The Great Escape*. Stalag Luft III was a large Prisoner of War (POW) camp near Sagan, Silesia. The prisoners held at Stalag Luft III were airmen of the British and American Air Forces. The camp grew to 60 acres and housed 10,000 allied airmen. The barracks were raised off the ground to make it easier to detect tunneling activities. The camp was located on land with very sandy subsoil that made it very difficult to construct tunnels. The sand was bright yellow and could easily be detected on clothing and on the ground outside the barracks. Additionally, the Germans placed seismograph microphones around the perimeter of the camp to detect any digging sounds below the surface.

The first successful escape occurred in October 1942 and was documented in two books. Flight Lieutenant Eric Williams, one of the three successful escapees wrote *The Goon in the Box*.

No Matter What You Can Do It

Another successful escapee, Flight Lieutenant Oliver Philpot, wrote his account of this escape in *The Stolen Journey*. The movie, *Trojan Horse*, was released in 1950.

The Trojan Horse was a gymnastic vaulting horse made of plywood. The horse concealed the men digging the hole, their tools and containers of dirt extracted from the hole. Prisoners would carry the horse to the same spot near the perimeter fence and conduct gymnastics exercises while the tunnel was dug below them. The noise and jumping concealed the sounds of the digging. At the end of the day, a wooden board was placed on the surface of the tunnel and covered with surface dirt. It took three prisoners, Lieutenant Michael Codner, Flight Lieutenant Eric Williams and Flight Lieutenant Oliver Philpot three months to dig a tunnel 100 feet long. Metal tubes through the tunnel roof provided air. No shoring was used to support the tunnel sides or roof. On the evening of October 29, 1942, Codner, Williams and Philpot made their escape. Two of them were able to reach the port of Stettin where they stowed away on a Danish ship and eventually made their way back to Britain. The other stowed away on a Swedish ship and was repatriated from Stockholm.

More memorable in recent years was the story of the escape that occurred on March 24, 1944. Seventy-Six Allied prisoners escaped through a 360-foot long tunnel. Seventy-three were recaptured and within two weeks, 50 of them were executed. The movie, *The Great Escape*, portrayed the planning, digging, escape and recapture. In January 1943, a South African-born Auxiliary Air Force pilot, Squadron Leader Roger Bushell, RAF, organized and led the famous escape from Stalag Luft III. The plan was to dig three tunnels – named 'Tom,' 'Dick,' and 'Harry.' Each tunnel entrance was contained inside the barracks buildings. The tunnels were dug 30 feet deep to evade the sound detection equipment along the fence perimeter. Each tunnel was two feet square. Larger chambers were dug to house equipment, workshops and staging posts inside the tunnels. Walls were shored up with wood from the prisoners' beds. As the tunnels grew in length, they devised methods to keep fresh air at the end of the tunnels for the workers. Eventually, electrical lighting was installed.

Rail lines were installed on the tunnel floor to transport dirt out of the tunnel. In a five-month period, over 130 tons of dirt was removed. Most of the tunnel dirt was stored in the barracks. When the barracks became overfilled, the dirt was disposed of on the surface outside the barracks by releasing it from inside the prisoners' trousers by using pouches made from socks. The dirt would fall to their feet and they would shuffle around the tunnel dirt with the surface dirt to hide it from being detected.

The volume of dirt quickly became a problem and they started storing the excess dirt in Tunnel 'Dick'. 'Dick' was also used to store the items needed by the escapees – maps, travel permits, compasses, clothing, etc. 'Tom' was discovered and shut down and every effort was expended to complete 'Harry'. 'Harry' was completed in March 1944. However, by then the American prisoners were moved to another Stalag.

The escape began at 5:00 a.m. on the morning of March 24th. The escapees found that they were just short of the trees even though the tunnel was nearly 360 feet long. Seventy-eight men crawled to freedom. The seventy-ninth man was seen by the guards emerging from the tunnel exit. Only five of the seventy-eight escapees evaded capture. The Germans took inventory of the barracks following the escape. They discovered many missing items: 4000 bed boards, 90 beds, 52 tables, 34 chairs, 76 benches, 1219 knives, 478 spoons, 69 lamps, 246 water cans, 30 shovels, 1000 feet of electrical wire, 600 feet of rope, 3424 towels, 1700 blankets and more than 1400 Red Cross milk cans.

Fifty of the seventy-three escapees were recaptured and shot. Seventeen of the twenty-three were returned to Stalag Luft III, four were sent to Sachsenhausen concentration camp and two were sent to Oflag IV-C Colditz. It is very interesting to note that the four escapees sent to Sachsenhausen managed to tunnel out past electric fences and double guards. Of the 76 escapees, only three were able to totally evade capture – Norwegians Per Bergsland, Jens Muller and Dutchman Bram van der Stok. After the war, the murder of the fifty escaped prisoners was one of the charges brought to the Nuremberg Trials.

Other noteworthy escapes during World War II were the escape of 131 French soldiers in September 1943 from Oflag XVII A Doellersheim; the escape of 300 prisoners from Sobibor in October 1943; and, the escape of 545 Japanese prisoners in August 1944 from Cowra, Australia.

All the **NO MATTER WHAT** escape decisions were made with the full realization that they may be executed upon recapture.

Summary:

Your 8th **NO MATTER WHAT** decision: Find a financial planner and discuss retirement options. If you have a retirement plan already, consider having a discussion with another financial planner and compare the results.

- **Guideline #104:** Consider Long-Term Care insurance – the younger you are the less expensive it is.

- **Guideline #105:** Plan your retirement for a minimum of 35 years.

- **Guideline #106:** Know what retirement lifestyle you really want – don't default into something because you didn't plan earlier enough for it.

- **Guideline #107:** You are the person in charge of your money.

- **Guideline #108**: Know what your time is worth. Make wise decisions how you spend your time.

- Affirmations must be present tense, positive and personal.

- Affirmations can change your self-image.

- The subconscious learns from rote memorization, from sensing, from experiences and from emotional attachments.

- The subconscious stores data for short-term and long-term retrieval.

- Your core self-belief system is generated from your emotional stockpile of data.

- The subconscious does not know the difference between garbage and fact.

- **Guideline #109:** Tell the subconscious what you want it to believe. Attach emotion and repeat it often.

- **Guideline #110:** Visualize your success daily.

- **Guideline #111:** Say your affirmations aloud.

- **Guideline #112:** Write your affirmations in longhand.

- Affirmations counter negativity.

- **Guideline #113:** Believe your affirmations.

- **Guideline #114:** Add **<u>NO MATTER WHAT</u>** to one or two of your important affirmations to add an extra emotion to your subconscious.
- **Guideline #115:** Say your affirmations before going to sleep.
- **Guideline #116:** Say your affirmations upon awakening.

"There are no secrets to success. It is the result of preparation, hard work and learning from failure." Colin Powell

"Try and fail, but don't try to fail." Stephen Kaggwa

"I didn't fail the test. I just found 100 ways to do it wrong." Benjamin Franklin

"Failure is the tuition you pay for success." Walter Brunell

"Don't wait. The time will never be right." Napoleon Hill

Personal Dashboard

Here is a thought for those who like to look at charts and graphs. Many companies have performance 'dashboards.' Senior management can look at their performance dashboards and tell, at a glance, if things are OK – in the green, so to speak. If problems exist, the dashboards will have those areas highlighted in red. The performance dashboard, for those unfamiliar with it, is like your car's dashboard with gauges and lights. It gives you a status of your car's systems. A company sets metrics for their performance dashboard and the results are calculated and transformed into a dashboard presentation.

Since you are the senior manager in your firm – why not consider having your own personal dashboard. It does not have to be elaborate, but it should give you a good idea of how things are running. Potential metrics for your personal dashboard could be:

- **Time for self**

- **Time for family**
- **Money for discretionary spending**
- **Money for savings/retirement**
- **Overall happiness**
- **Control over your distractions**
- **Total debt remaining**
- **% Milestones made on time over last year**

Your personal dashboard does not have to be elaborate or detailed. It should not take you very long to prepare it, and it does not have to have a gauge-like appearance or have red and green colors. It is something for those inclined to know where they are at a moment's glance.

Typically, a person works for a company and his or her paycheck comes from that company. You work and you are paid. It is rare when someone works for a company and becomes financially independent over time.

Robert Kiyosaki in his book, *Cashflow Quadrant" Rich Dad's Guide to Financial Freedom*, developed an excellent model of cash flow in businesses. The **Cashflow Quadrant** is a conceptual tool to explain how money is earned. The **Cashflow Quadrant** is represented by four quadrants formed by a large **'plus sign'** with the letter **'E'** in the top left quadrant, the letter **'B'** in the top right quadrant, the letter '**S**' in the bottom left quadrant, and the letter '**I**' in the bottom right quadrant.

E	B
S	I

Robert Kiyosaki's Cash Flow Quadrant

'E' is for the Employer

Cash flows <u>from</u> the employer <u>to</u> the employee. The employee <u>does not own</u> the business. The employee works and is paid. An 'E' employee can be the president of the company or the mail clerk. The security in the 'E' quadrant comes from the company providing employment, benefits and opportunity for growth.

'S' is for the Self-Employed

Cash flows similarly <u>from</u> the company to the employee, but <u>you are the owner</u> of the business. You take the risks. Security rests on how good you are and how responsive you are to the changes in your business environment. Typically, you will find doctors, lawyers, accountants, mechanics, decorators, etc. in the Self-Employed group. The Self-Employed can and usually have employees working for them. History has shown that 80% of all businesses fail within the first five years. Of those 20% remaining, another 80% will fail within the next five years.

'B' is for the Business Owner

It is a step up from the Self-Employed. It is usually determined by the number of employees you have working for you. Robert Kiyosaki states that to be in the 'B' quadrant you should employ over <u>500 people</u>. The real difference between the 'B' and an 'S' quadrants is that the owner in the 'B' quadrant <u>can leave</u> his business for an extended period and still get paid based on the results of his employees. The 'S' quadrant owner is usually so critical to that business that an absence for an extended time could force the closure of that business.

'I' is for the Investor

The bulk of the money generated in this business is from investments. The primary difference between the 'I' quadrant and 'E' quadrant is that income is generated from personal investing knowledge in the 'I' quadrant. Investments can be in many things, such as gold, real estate, stocks, bonds, etc.

Success in one quadrant does not guarantee success in another. Why? It requires a **different mindset** to be **successful** in each quadrant. Security and financial freedom also vary in each of the quadrants. As you move from the 'E' quadrant to the 'S' quadrant to the 'B' quadrant and finally to the 'I' quadrant your security and financial freedom increase.

Can you jump from the 'E' quadrant to the 'I' quadrant? Certainly! Attain the **requisite knowledge**, take the **risks**, make the **investments** and build your **'I'** quadrant business. Break free from having a boss and take those extended trips you have been dreaming of most of your life.

Most of you are programmed to work in the '**E**' quadrant. How many times have you heard, '**Go to school, get good grades, find a good company and work hard**.' Sometimes you might have heard, 'If you want to be rich, become a doctor or a lawyer.' However, the reality is - if you want financial freedom you must become a <u>business owner</u> – that's the '**B**' quadrant and then an investor – the '**I**' quadrant. Robert Kiyosaki said that the difference between the '**S**' quadrant and the '**B**' quadrant was the number of employees – at least, 500.

So how can I possibly start a business and hire 500 employees? Start out incrementally and look at the options you have. Large businesses begin small and grow. Start with something you can do while you are working in the '**E**' quadrant. Buy a parking lot or a car wash and start your business that way. It requires an investment to get started, but it is something relatively simple. What about real estate or stock trading? Do you have the requisite knowledge to start in either of those fields? Probably not, but that does not mean you cannot get it. If that is your dream, then it is attainable. There is a lot of low-cost and free information about those fields. There are risks associated with both – a downturn in the housing market, or a slump in the stock market for example. Nevertheless, money is made in both up and down markets if you know what to do, when, and are willing to take those risks.

Maybe you have specialized knowledge and can become a consultant. It is a bit more difficult to start because of the time constraints of having to work in the '**E**' quadrant. You can work at nights and on weekends and build websites, mentor students, create interior designs, etc. What do all these options have in common while you are working in the '**E**' quadrant? They all start out as <u>home businesses</u>. As a home business, you have tremendous tax advantages that the employee in the '**E**' quadrant <u>does not have</u>.

Robert Kiyosaki has written many books and developed games to hone your skills in making financial decisions. Robert Kiyosaki truly believes that you must <u>increase your financial literacy to obtain wealth</u> – you must be a business owner or investor to generate passive income.

Some people risk life and limb to live free. Their **NO MATTER WHAT** decision is so firmly ingrained in their mind that there is no other option. A good example of this is found in the movie *Papillon* that highlighted the escape attempts of convicted felon and fugitive Henri Charriere. I have seen the movie and read two of Henri Charriere's books. The word *Papillon* is 'butterfly' in French, and was based on the tattoo on Henri's chest. Henri Charriere was sentenced to hard labor at Devil's Island penal colony. After arriving at Devil's Island, Henri faked illness and was sent to the infirmary. He and two others managed to escape by sailboat. The wind quit and they were caught off the Columbian coast. Henri escaped from the Columbian prison and traveled to the Guajira peninsula. He assimilated into a coastal village and married two teenage sisters.

No Matter What You Can Do It

Henri left the village intent on revenge upon those who wrongfully imprisoned him. He was shortly captured and imprisoned at Santa Marta and then transferred to Barranquilla. A short while later he was extradited back to the Devil's Island penal colony in French Guiana. Henri was sentenced to two years of solitary confinement as punishment for his earlier escape from Devil's Island. The two years of solitary confinement were on Ile Saint-Joseph, an island 11 kilometers off the French Guiana coast. After two years of solitary confinement, Henri was transferred to Royal Island. He attempted to escape again and was returned to solitary confinement – this time for eight years. His original sentence of eight years was reduced to eighteen months because he risked his life to save the life of a girl caught in shark-infested waters.

The penalty for escape was death after the beginning of World War II. Henri feigned insanity and was sent to an insane asylum on Royal Island. He reasoned that insane prisoners could not be sentenced to death for any reason. Royal Island was lightly guarded. Henri attempted to escape again, and his boat crashed on the rocks and he was nearly killed. Henri was deemed to be 'cured' of his insanity and he requested that he be transferred to Devil's Island. Henri studied the waters around the island and discovered an inlet where he could predict the ocean currents. He experimented by throwing sacks of coconuts into the inlet. Every seventh wave would force the coconuts out to sea far enough to drift to the mainland. The first six waves always caused the coconuts to be smashed on the rocks below.

Henri and another inmate tied coconuts together with sack material. They jumped with the coconut sacks into the inlet below when the seventh wave approached. They drifted for days surviving only on coconut milk and pulp. Upon landing on the mainland, Henri narrowly escaped being swallowed by a large pit of quicksand. He eventually made his way to Georgetown, Guyana. Henri was not content to remain a 'free' man in Guyana. He continued his journey to Venezuela. He was captured again and imprisoned at El Dorado. He survived his prison sentence and eventually became a Venezuelan citizen.

Summary:

- You do not own the business in the '**E**' Quadrant. You are the employee. The company assumes all the risk.

- You own the business in the '**S**' Quadrant. You assume all the business risk. You may hire other employees – they become '**E**' Quadrant workers.

- You own the business in the '**B**' Quadrant. The difference is the size of the company and the necessity of the '**S**' Quadrant owner to be present nearly 100% of the time. **'B'** Quadrant owners may not have to be present nearly 100% of the time.

- The **'I'** Quadrant owner uses his/her personal knowledge of financial investing to build the business.
- Business owners have greater tax benefits than employees working for a company.
- 80% of all businesses fail in the first five years.
- 80% of the remaining businesses fail in the next five years. Four out a hundred survive ten years in business.
- **Guideline #117:** Seriously look at the benefits of starting a home-based business. The tax advantages generally outweigh the income for the first few years.

"Success is going from failure to failure without losing enthusiasm." Winston Churchill

"Know where the information is and use it. That's the secret to success." Albert Einstein

"Strive not to be a success, but of value." Albert Einstein

"Success is falling nine times and getting up ten." Bon Jovi

"The key to change is to let go of fear." Roxanne Cash

"I have been impressed with the urgency of doing. Knowing is not enough; we must apply. Being willing is not enough; we must do." Leonardo de Vinci

Additional Business Opportunities

Many things that you spend money on daily are not deductible for the employee in the '**E**' quadrant. But, if you <u>own a home business</u> you can deduct business mileage, business meals, and other costs associated with your business – such as internet service, postage, paper, software, books, etc. You can also deduct the cost of your business operations, such as electricity, insurance, maintenance and upkeep – based on the space you use in your home. If you use **5%** of your home for your office and storage, then you can deduct **5%** of the appropriate business operating expenses. Business trips are also deductible. You have many more deductions compared to an employee in the '**E**' quadrant taking the same trip.

As a <u>home business owner,</u> you are also entitled to many other deductions, one of the most interesting is medical and dental care. Consult an accountant, one who specializes in home businesses, to determine what and how to qualify for this deduction, and how much is deductible. It is very important to get the right accountant – one who specializes in home businesses. It is not unreasonable to assume that if you earn $200 a month profit in your home business that you might be able to deduct $500 or more a month in legitimate business expenses - which means a much larger income tax return for you <u>to invest in your future</u>. Many of your expenses are part of your normal monthly expenses anyway.

There is another kind of business opportunity that **everyone can own**. Robert Kiyosaki tells us that <u>network marketing</u> should be given serious consideration for employees in the 'E' quadrant who want to transition to the 'B' quadrant. Robert Kiyosaki says that the network marketing businesses are designed to expand to well over 500 people.

The income potential in the 'E' and 'S' quadrants is limited by what you can do by yourself. The income potential in network marketing is not limited by what you can do by yourself – it is based on what your business organization can do – like a 'B' quadrant business.

A network marketing business is one that is <u>less costly to start</u> compared to buying a parking lot or a car wash. The requisite knowledge to start is less than a realtor, stockbroker, or web designer. Generally, the entry-level requirements for most network marketing businesses are:

- **Low cost – usually less than $500.**
- **You must want to do it**
- **You must be coachable.**

Successful network marketing business owners have developed systems and tools for new business owners to use and follow. You can also leave your business to your family or create a legacy for future generations. I personally think this is a major consideration to own any kind of business. Most network marketing businesses are full of positive people wanting to make a difference in their lives.

Like all businesses, you must do the right things at the right time. If you think it is worth considering, then do your research before selecting one.

- Talk to the people in various network marketing companies to find out as much as you can.
- Do not pre-judge one over another - be objective in your evaluation.
- Select something that makes sense to you and something for which you have a passion.
- Ensure that the network marketing industry you are interested in is growing.
- You also want to ensure that the network marketing company has competent and stable management.

No Matter What You Can Do It

Remember that most businesses <u>fail in the first five years</u> – look carefully at the record of accomplishment of your potential company. If it has only been around for a year, then you might want to continue looking. Yes, there are success stories every day, but statistics tell us that most do not. There are research resources for you to analyze opportunities in network marketing. One book I recommend to people considering a network marketing opportunity is, *How to Select a Network Marketing Company, Six Keys to Scrutinizing, Comparing and Selecting a Million Dollar Home-Based Business*, by Daren C. Falter.

Once you have decided to start your home business, whether it is a network marketing business or not – **start with your business plan**.

- Define what you expect your business to do.
- Project your <u>income</u> into the future as well as your <u>expenses</u>.
    - o Minimum three to five years
- Define <u>how</u> you are going to do your business – how you are going to <u>market</u> it and <u>advertise</u> it.
- Treat as a business!
- Develop your <u>personal growth plan</u> to align your knowledge and ability with your business as it develops. You must grow with your business!
- Set up a tax file for your business expenses and income.

- Work at least 45 minutes to an hour a day on the average. Income tax regulations are very strict regarding hobbies and businesses. A hobby of selling things on eBay can easily become a business with the right <u>mindset</u>, <u>planning</u>, <u>documentation</u> and <u>records</u>.

It has been observed by industry analysts that network marketing business owners who concentrate on the product/service generally **do not have** the same income potential as network marketing business owners who concentrate on developing business leaders within their business. Business owners concentrating on products and services only generally make less than $1000 a month. If you are 'leveraging' your business as Robert Kiyosaki tells us that successful business owners do, then you can earn more income based on those working for you.

If you want more than a $1000 a month coming in from your network marketing business, you need to concentrate on the <u>quality of the person you are transitioning into your business</u>. You want someone primarily <u>interested in building their business</u>, rather than someone primarily interested in the product/service side. These kinds of people are harder to find, but you have a greater return on your business. Normally you might find **three out of a hundred** who fit in this category.

No Matter What You Can Do It

As part of your research, you should be asking successful network marketing business owners – *how do you recruit people into your network marketing business*? How do you know you are recruiting a business builder? How can you tell if the business builder is productive? How effective is your system in creating successful business builders? **Remember you are one hiring the company – not the other way around**. Make the right decision! Monitor that decision over time. Do not assume that you will be making big money your first or second year. It is possible, but not the norm. Prepare to spend at least **five to seven years** to see your income competitive with your 'E' quadrant job. Incremental adjustments along the way make the difference. Treat it as a business and do not give up because the **fog is covering the road as you are going up the hill**. Use other business owners in your network marketing business to learn the business and to keep a positive mental attitude!

- **Do not start without having adequate mentoring, education and training.**
- **Frustration will set in quickly and thoughts of 'quitting' will permeate your psyche. Do your research.**
- **Understand attrition and retention factors for your potential business.**
- **Select carefully what you want.**

- **Get the skills needed to be successful in that business.**
- **Begin cautiously and deliberately.**
- **Measure your progress and understand why you are gaining or losing ground on your goals.**

James Arnold "Hoot" Johnson lived a hard life as a young man. He did not graduate from high school or pass a GED. In his early twenties, Hoot worked as a Hot Lineman (working on live electrical lines) for L. L. Flowers Construction Company. One day while working atop a 25' pole with 72,000 volts, he fell backward and should have let his safety line save him, but he did not. He grabbed a nearby electrical line to break his fall. He was wearing three pairs of gloves – each provided a different level of protection from electrical shock/burn. Almost instantly, Hoot lost all his fingers on his right hand, and fell further and landed on top of another power line with it across his waist. This time his safety harness prevented him from falling further. It took a while to rescue Hoot, but he was still alive.

Through many surgeries, Hoot ended up losing one arm and both his legs. He was still a young man with a family. He did not accept his status in life resulting from his accident. He made a **NO MATTER WHAT** decision to work and provide for his family's needs. After six months of surgeries and rehabilitation, Hoot returned to work. There was limited compensation from his injuries and his company offered him a minimum wage job that led to becoming a purchasing agent with the company.

One of his many **NO MATTER WHAT** decisions was to walk. He traveled to Houston to be measured for new prosthetic devices for his legs. He was measured for them, but not shown how to attach them or how to walk in them. When Hoot got home, he figured out how to put them on and how to stand in them. Within an hour, he walked out of his bedroom. It was this type of energy – sheer willpower - that Hoot put into everything he did.

Hoot knew he needed to learn new things to advance in his company. He was very creative and saw things others could not see. One significant success story was the ability of his company to do underground water construction along with underground electrical construction. This type of thinking eventually led Hoot to form his own company. Hoot became very proficient in every job he had. He could process job costs in his head just by looking at the lay of the land. He knew how much piping it would take, the cost of drilling, valves and all other related costs without prints or schematics. He could quote a job on the spot – and be right every time. He was well respected by his work crews and they produced quality work.

The fuel crisis opened a door for Hoot in the mid-70's. He applied his creative thinking to apply his company's water removal ability and equipment to the oil/gas industry. He approached both his management and oil companies about his vision and a new division of his company was formed. Thus, under Hoot's leadership, L. L. Flowers became the largest rural water construction company in the state of Texas.

In 1982, Hoot joined Rhode Construction Company and furthered his knowledge and experience in water removal from oil fields. In 1996, Hoot and his three oldest sons opened Hoot Johnson Construction Company and eventually transitioned from utility services to oilfield services exclusively.

Hoot loved to share himself with others – especially those in need. He provided support and encouragement to patients in hospitals where he touched many lives. He was always compassionate, caring, helpful and generous to those in need of physical, spiritual and emotional needs. When Hoot was in his early twenties, he owned a 900 square-foot mobile home. At his death, Hoot was a self-made millionaire. He and his sons all owned 4000-5000 square foot homes. He was always very generous to those who helped him throughout his life.

Hoot had a wonderful personality – he could disarm strangers with his smile and manner of speaking. A tribute to his personality was shown during his funeral in September 2008 in which 3,000 people from around the country attended – many who never had met him. He made his **NO MATTER WHAT** decision and rose from adversity and used his will power and entrepreneurial spirit to reach out and touch thousands of people during his life.

Summary:

Guideline # 118: Always get an accountant who specializes in home-based businesses.

The 'E' and 'S' Quadrant limit your income to the amount of time you invest.

Network marketing businesses provide an opportunity for unlimited income because they are not dependent on the amount of time you invest.

Network marketing businesses generally are less costly to start compared to other businesses.

Network marketing businesses allow you to leave a legacy to your family.

Network marketing businesses have medical and dental tax advantages.

Guideline # 119: Don't prejudge people or opportunities.

Guideline # 120: Keep your passion in the things you do.

Guideline #121: Select a business in an industry that is growing.

Guideline # 122: Develop a business plan as soon as you can. Project your income and expenses for at least five years.

Guideline # 123: Start a tax file before you start your business.

Guideline # 124: Develop your communication skills. They are critical to any business you choose.

Guideline # 125: Treat your business as a business always.

Guideline # 126: Grow with your business. Ensure you get the education and training necessary to be better than your competitors. Do what your competitors won't do to stay ahead of the game.

Guideline # 127: Work your business daily. Keep records of what you are doing. The records will help you determine what you need to change to improve more.

Guideline # 128: Plan to spend at least five to seven years to earn enough money in your business to replace your regular job.

Guideline # 129: Get a business mentor.

Guideline # 130: Give to others as you can – emotionally, spiritually and physically. Be concerned more with giving rather than getting from others.

Guideline # 131: Be generous to all those who help you.

"There is no fear in love, but perfect love casteth out fear…"
1 John 4:18

"The most important sale in life is to sell yourself to yourself."
Maxwell Maltz

No Matter What You Can Do It

"The best way to predict the future is to create it." Peter Drucker

"The only thing we know about the future is that it is going to be different." Peter Drucker

"God places the heaviest burden on those who can carry its weight." Reggie White

"If we're growing, we're always out of our comfort zone." John Maxwell

AUTHOR BIOGRAPHY

F. M. 'Red' O'Laughlin, III, is a researcher, author, public speaker and master educator. He speaks on health and wellness, aging, personal growth and motivation. Red states often that, *"If you treat symptoms, you will always treat symptoms. You must treat the cause of a problem to correct it."* Red researches what happens at the cellular level in the human body, biochemically speaking. He looks for cause and effect relationships. He identifies causes of health problems. He writes and speaks about those causes and the potential options for correcting those problems.

Red's professional civilian specialties are quality assurance, reliability engineering and logistics. He has worked in senior management positions at National Semiconductor, Memorex, Dresser Industries, NL Industries, Boeing, and Halliburton. He has written thousands of documents (procedures, policies, instructions, technical articles and reports). He has trained thousands in the military, academic and corporate levels.

No Matter What You Can Do It

Red has an A. A. in Quality Assurance from De Anza College, a B. S. in Chemistry from Texas A&I University, an M. S. in Systems Management from the University of Southern California, an M. B. A. from the University of Houston and is a graduate of the Naval War College and the Defense Resource Management Institute. He is a Certified Quality Engineer, Certified Reliability Engineer, Certified Quality Manager and a Certified Professional Logistician. He is a Certified Lead Assessor for ISO-9000 and a Certified TapRooT Assessor. Red is a Distinguished Toastmaster (DTM) with Toastmasters International.

Red has written and published *Failure Is Not an Option*, a book on goal setting, *RESULTS MATTER When You Want to Lose Weight and Keep It Off,* and *Longevity Secrets for Health Aging – How to Live to 100 Years of Age with the Body of a Healthy 50-Year-Old and the Mind of a 25-Year-Old.*

Red retired as a Naval Captain with 31 years in the Navy Reserves. He was a Naval Flight Officer and flew nearly one thousand flights in the P-3 antisubmarine warfare aircraft. Red was invited to Vietnam at the beginning of his Navy career and joined the Navy Reserves after four plus years of active duty. He went back on active duty for six years after twenty years in the Naval Reserve and retired as the Deputy Director of Reserve Affairs in Stuttgart, Germany. In that position, Red was responsible for oversight of 5,500 Reservists in 89 countries in Europe and Africa. Red has traveled to 60 countries during his military career.

No Matter What You Can Do It

Captain O'Laughlin has been awarded the Defense Superior Service Medal, Defense Meritorious Service Medal, Meritorious Service Medal, Air Medal with numeral '1', Joint Service Commendation Medal, Navy Marine Corps Commendation Medal (2 awards), Joint Meritorious Unit Award (2 awards), Navy Unit Commendation, Meritorious Unit Commendation, Coast Guard Meritorious Unit Commendation (with Operational Distinction) and the National Defense Service Medal (two awards). Additionally, he has numerous campaign and service awards.

Red and Marilyn have been married for over 47 years and have two children and three grandchildren. He is the owner of MRO Global, LLC.

Please note - This book was originally published in 2010 in physical form only for sale at seminars. It is being update (slightly) and republished in 2017 in electronic and physical formats.

Contact Information

Red O'Laughlin

3106 Indian Wells Court

Missouri City, TX 77459-3461

281-437-8114 W

281-687-1188 C

red.olaughlin@gmail.com

www.redolaughlin.com/

www.facebook.com/red.olaughlin

www.linkedin.com/in/red-olaughlin/

www.instagram.com/red.olaughlin/

Made in the USA
Lexington, KY
14 January 2018